Multimodal Teaching and Learning

BLOOMSBURY CLASSICS IN LINGUISTICS

Multimodal Teaching and Learning, *Gunther Kress,
Carey Jewitt, Jon Ogborn and Charalampos Tsatsarelis*
Opposition in Discourse, *Lesley Jeffries*
Second Language Identities, *David Block*
Worlds of Written Discourse, *Vijay Bhatia*

More titles coming soon!

Multimodal Teaching and Learning

The Rhetorics of the Science Classroom

GUNTHER KRESS, CAREY JEWITT, JON OGBORN AND CHARALAMPOS TSATSARELIS

B L O O M S B U R Y

LONDON · NEW DELHI · NEW YORK · SYDNEY

Bloomsbury Academic

An imprint of Bloomsbury Publishing Plc

50 Bedford Square
London
WC1B 3DP
UK

1385 Broadway
New York
NY 10018
USA

www.bloomsbury.com

Bloomsbury is a registered trade mark of Bloomsbury Publishing Plc

First published 2001 by Continuum International Publishing Group

Bloomsbury Classics in Linguistics edition first published in 2014
by Bloomsbury Academic

© Gunther Kress, Carey Jewitt, Jon Ogborn and Charalampos Tsatsarelis
2001, 2014

Gunther Kress, Carey Jewitt, Jon Ogborn and Charalampos Tsatsarelis have
asserted their right under the Copyright, Designs and Patents Act, 1988,
to be identified as the Authors of this work.

British Library Cataloguing-in-Publication Data
A catalogue record for this book is available from the British Library.

ISBN: PB: 978-1-4725-2271-9
ePDF: 978-1-4725-7104-5
ePub: 978-1-4725-7105-2

Library of Congress Cataloging-in-Publication Data
A catalog record for this book is available from the Library of Congress.

Typeset by Deanta Global Publishing Services, Chennai, India
Printed and bound in India

Contents

List of Figures

List of Tables

Foreword

The interdisciplinarity and the problem-based focus of applied linguistics generally, and of this new series in particular, are well evidenced in this first contribution, *Multimodal Teaching and Learning: The Rhetorics of the Science Classroom*. Drawing on an extended research project into the nature of multimodality and the rhetorics of the science classroom, the authors explore how science teachers present subject matter and seek to shape their students' understanding of it through the interactive processes of classroom teaching and learning. Such an exploration inevitably involves Kress and his colleagues in a task which goes beyond description of the language of the science classroom *per se*. Any linguistic description can only be a partial account of such processes. The point of departure for the authors is that communication in science classrooms must involve the mapping of all representational and communicative resources available to teachers and learners: hence their multimodal stance towards the analysis of situated interaction in the science classroom. The project accordingly brings together scholars with backgrounds in the analysis of discourse and their colleagues in science education to address the pedagogical representation and mediation of discipline-specific school-based knowledge. The book is well-founded theoretically and methodologically. The authors propose a multimodal view of language as communication within a broad social semiotic approach, and link this with a dynamic view of the teaching and learning of science.

Mainstream classroom research has until recently focused, not surprisingly, on the role played by language in describing learning processes and evaluating learning outcomes. Seen from this language-centred perspective, the language of other subjects and classroom settings, such as science, geography, economics or business, assumes the status of a specialized register or genre. Describing such subject-specific language has attracted the attention of many applied linguists, for example, the collected papers in Martin and Veel (1998). In a sense, the task of linguistic descriptions of subject-specific classroom settings assumes a 'language learning' perspective on the acquisition of subject-specific knowledge. That is to say, competence in a subject such as geography or economics becomes equated with one's ability to acquire the languages of geography and economics, respectively. Lemke's (1990) claim that 'learning science means learning to *talk* science' is illustrative here. Such a language-centred view of subject knowledge, while useful in accounting for genre-specific differences across subjects, is bound to overlook all other aspects of 'knowledgeable action' (cf. Goodwin's [1992] broader account of professional vision which integrates ways of *saying* with ways of *seeing,* and Hak's [1999] general point about talk bias in professional discourse studies).

The distinctive contribution of Gunther Kress and his colleagues in their study of science classrooms is to broaden this language-centred focus in order to examine, firstly, the interface between language and other modalities of communication, and, secondly, to do so in conjunction with a study of the interpretive practices that science educators and science teachers bring into play in managing lessons. Doing so enables them to reach beyond genre-analytic accounts of the language of science, and to set their goal as interpreting the rhetorics of the science classroom. The notion of 'rhetoric' here also extends beyond argumentation realized through language form. We see this as an extension of Cicourel's (1992) notion of ecological validity, whereby classroom activity is interpreted as language *and* as action, in relation to other modes of communicative resources which participants draw upon to negotiate meaning and achieve understanding.

This book thus transcends the traditionally language-focused gaze of some applied linguists. This does not imply, however, that by adopting a multimodal paradigm the role language plays in the educational domain is diminished. Rather, language attains a more relational status as far as the distribution of communicative load is concerned. This is what is referred to as *affordances* that each mode offers in getting things done. According to Kress and his colleagues: 'Language is not absent from our discussion, but nor is it central. It is, as we have said, "there", but "there" among all other modes: foregrounded when it *is,* in the representational ensemble, and not foregrounded in our descriptions when it is not so in the data.' The so-called extralinguistic stuff is no longer a residual category, peripheral to the analytic act of describing the phenomenon under study. It reminds us that science classrooms should be seen as a cultural setting with their own semiotic systems where certain types of knowledge are produced, distributed and reinforced, similar to what happens in other work-related settings (Engstrom and Middleton, 1997; Heath and Luff, 2000).

As an alternative to seeing classroom activity from different disciplinary perspectives what we have here is a pluralization of the object of inquiry. In the current climate, there is an over-indulgence in inter- and trans-disciplinary approaches whereby scholars from different disciplines make an attempt to contribute 'something extra' to explain the phenomenon under study. What Kress and his fellow authors accomplish is a broadening of the phenomenon of the science classroom, supported by an analytic focus which allows them to consider language in conjunction with action. In this regard, the multimodal approach taken in this book resembles a projection in *re-specification,* similar to the ethnomethodological turn in sociological inquiry embodied in Garfinkel (1967) – turning away from normative rules and norms of social behaviour to the accomplishment of practical action.

A different view of language leads to a different view of learning. For Kress and his colleagues, 'learning can no longer be treated as a process which depends on language centrally, or even dominantly'. Learning is thus much more than a matter of speaking or writing the language of science; it is a 'dynamic process of transformative sign-making'.

One consequence of this re-orientation is that the authors are enabled to consider the activities of the classroom in their entirety, offering the possibility of more holistic analyses of 'what actually happens' in classrooms (e.g., activities of experiment, demonstration, analogy, etc.) rather than a narrowly defined focus on 'what we are interested in analysing' (e.g., language). Such a stance is not only likely to be more revealing of classroom practices but more likely to appeal to those teachers and students whose activities we seek to understand. We may say that a multimodal approach is understanding-oriented in two senses of the term: how the participants understand their actions of doing teaching and learning; and how analysts seek to understand this co-produced, context-bound activity. This comes closer to aligning participants' and analysts' perspectives on the object of inquiry, rather than imposing one's motivated lookings (Sarangi and Candlin, 2001). Because participation is always constituted in multimodal action, the multimodal approach to research adopted by the authors as a means of illuminating the ongoingness of classroom activity is not only harmonious and apt, but provides a classic instance of 'reciprocity of perspectives'.

In addition to its theoretical innovativeness, the book demonstrates methodologically how to conduct collaborative, interdisciplinary project research. More specifically, the authors find ways of integrating linguistic and visual data in their analysis of classroom action. The very specificity of the account offered in this book is one of its main strengths, as is the way the authors have refrained from making value judgements about what counts as good and bad practice. In agreeing with them that a good description – 'thick description' in Geertz's terms – should serve as a useful resource for thinking about science pedagogy and practice, there is clearly some way to go before we can identify effective models of classroom communication for raising science teachers' awareness through professional development. We should note also that a multimodal view of communication can be extended to the analysis of other classroom settings and other forms of classroom interaction. After all, it is not only science classrooms that are constituted in multimodality and not only science teachers who make use of different communicative resources for 'the business of doing science'. Multimodality is what constitutes language classrooms as well, if only we were to shift our analytic gaze from language. Similarly, situated teacher–student encounters and interactions among students in paired or groupwork settings are not mediated only in and through language but involve other semiotic modes. More generally, our understanding of what goes on in a science classroom is not all that different from the social construction of scientific knowledge (Latour, 1987; Latour and Woolgar, 1979).

This book not only forms a basis for further cross-disciplinary inquiry into the co-production of scientific knowledge and practice both inside and outside the classroom setting, but has considerable relevance for widening the scope of applied linguistics. As the authors themselves make plain: 'We feel that in order to newly and properly understand language we need to step outside it, and take a satellite view of it. We hope that our book says more, by implication, about language, whether as speech or as writing, than do many other books which have "language" centrally as their focus.'

Christopher N. Candlin
Centre for English Language Education and
Communication Research
City University of Hong Kong

Srikant Sarangi
Centre for Language and Communication Research
Cardiff University

References

Cicourel, A. V. (1992) 'The interpretation of communicative contexts: examples from medical encounters', in A. Duranti and C. Goodwin (eds), *Rethinking Context: Language as an Interactive Phenomenon.* Cambridge: Cambridge University Press, pp. 291–310.

Engstrom, Y. and Middleton, D. (eds) (1997) *Cognition and Communication at Work.* Cambridge: Cambridge University Press.

Garfinkel, H. (1967) *Studies in Ethnomethodology.* Englewood Cliffs, NJ: Prentice Hall.

Goodwin, C. (1992) 'Professional vision', *American Anthropologist,* 96(3):606–33.

Hak, T. (1999) '"Text" and "con-text": talk bias in studies of health care work', in S. Sarangi and C. Roberts (eds), *Talk, Work and Institutional Order: Discourse in Medical, Mediation and Management Settings.* Berlin: Mouton de Gruyter, pp. 427–51.

Heath, C. and Luff, P. (2000) *Technology in Action.* Cambridge: Cambridge University Press.

Latour, B. (1987) *Science in Action.* Cambridge, MA: Harvard University Press.

Latour, B. and Woolgar, S. (1979) *Laboratory Life: The Social Construction of Scientific Facts.* Beverley Hills: Sage.

Lemke, J. (1990) *Talking Science: Language, Learning and Values.* Norwood: Ablex.

Martin, J. R. and Veel, R. (eds) (1998) *Reading Science: Critical and Functional Perspectives.* London: Routledge.

Sarangi, S. and Candlin, C. N. (2001) '"Motivational relevancies": some methodological reflections on social theoretical and sociolinguistic practice', in N. Coupland, S. Sarangi and C. N. Candlin (eds), *Sociolinguistic and Social Theory.* London: Pearson Education.

Acknowledgements

This work would not have been possible without the teachers who do these things, who are the accomplished rhetors, these orchestrators of incredibly rich arrangements, and the students, whose energy, inventiveness, enthusiasm and sheer intelligence we came to witness through the research, and have attempted to reflect in our accounts. We would like to thank these teachers and students (and the schools as institutions), who are often under unbearable pressures of all kinds, for giving us access to the classrooms, and the complex activities they are engaged in. We hope this book stands in part as a refutation of the jeremiads and hostilities heaped on schools, students and teachers. Nor would the work have been possible without the support of an ESRC grant, 'The Rhetorics of the Science Classroom: A Multicultural Approach' (R000236931).

We have also benefited much from interaction, comment, advice, and critique from many friends and colleagues, notably, Theo van Leeuwen, Andrew Brown, Jan Derry, Paul Dowling, Anton Franks, Joan Leach, Radan Martinec, Greg Myers, Mary Scott and Phil Scott, and the supportive environment of the two academic groups Culture Communication and Societies, and Science and Technology.

Introduction

This book takes a new look at some old questions surrounding teaching and learning. It does this in two ways. First, whereas much traditional classroom research has focused on language – the teacher's speech, the students' speech in response, the written texts used in teaching and learning – this book takes an approach in which the multiplicity of *modes of communication* that are active in the classroom are given equally serious attention. As a consequence language – whether as speech or as writing – becomes simply one of several *modes* through which the business of science is done, by the teacher or by the students. We use the term *multimodality* to describe that approach. Second, a serious look at the multiplicity of modes, which are always and simultaneously in use, shows conclusively that meaning resides in all of them and that each contributes to the overall meaning of the multimodal ensemble in quite specific ways.

This realization has profound consequences for views of learning: learning can no longer be treated as a process which depends on language centrally, or even dominantly. Our data reveals conclusively that meaning is made in all modes separately, and at the same time, that meaning is an effect of all the modes acting jointly. Learning happens through (or to put it as we see it – learners actively engage with) all modes as a complex activity in which speech or writing are involved among a number of modes.

Several issues open out from this starting-point: if there are a number of distinct modes in operation at the same time (in our description and analysis we focus on speech, image, gesture, action with models, writing, etc.), then the first question is: 'Do they offer differing possibilities for representing?' For ourselves we put that question in these terms: 'What are the *affordances* of each mode used in the science classroom; what are the potentials and limitations for representing of each mode?'; and, 'Are the modes specialized to function in particular ways. Is speech, let's say, best for this, and image best for that?'

This is quite a new question and it is not merely a recasting of the realization, which has of course always been there, that there are 'extra-linguistic' forms of communication. The question is new not only because 'extra-linguistic' becomes an unusable term (since it is based on conceptions of language as central and other modes as existing merely in the periphery), but because in principle at least it says that image may, at a particular moment, be as fully representational as speech, or even more so; that speech may be relatively backgrounded while image is in the foreground. It also changes the job of making representations. When it was thought that language was really all there is, the issue of representation could plausibly be seen as one of using the code of speech or writing simply to 'encode' the meaning. Now the question has become much more complex: 'If there are these various modes, and they have different affordances, which mode shall I use for what purpose?'

Making a representation now goes well beyond simple encoding. It has become a matter of active, deliberate *design*, and meaning-making becomes a matter of the individual's active shaping and reshaping of the resources that he or she has available, in the wish to make representations match intentions as closely as possible.

Theoretically speaking, the discipline which is relevant to that enterprise is now no longer linguistics, which can offer a partial account only, but semiotics, which deals with signs in all forms and with the meaning made in all modes. The central term in semiotics is the *sign,* an entity consisting of a form fused with a meaning (a *signifier* fused with a *signified*). Signs exist in the wide variety of material forms which a culture (or a group within a culture) decides are to be used in the representation of the meanings of that culture. 'Science' and 'Science Education' may form one such culture.

In the following section, we briefly outline the theoretical framework of social semiotics within which our multimodal approach to the making of meaning in the science classroom is set.

Representation and communication

In the traditional approach to communication and representation, which we shall characterize as *monomodal* (misleadingly, because communication has always been multimodal), the commonly held assumption was that articulate, rationally based representation and communication took place through the medium of language (the differentiation of speech and writing as distinct modes was not an insight of the monomodal approach) and consequently theories of communication were identical to all intents and purposes with theories of language. Articulate representation was by means of language; full communication was made possible by means of language. The obverse of this situation was one in which other forms of representation (both the so-called extra-linguistic, paralinguistic forms as well as modes such as image and gesture) were described in terms taken over from linguistic theories. After all, if language was seen as the central, even the only, rational form of communication, then it would be obvious that the terms describing *its* structure would serve adequately to describe communicational characteristics of other forms of communication.

By contrast, our approach holds that communication is inevitably multimodal and that it is a mistake to take the descriptive terminology of linguistics and apply it to modes which are distinct in their materiality from speech or writing. We assume that the descriptive framework has to be derived from the specific characteristics of the mode itself. For instance, the temporal succession of elements in speech leads to one set of possibilities for representing, whereas the spatial simultaneity of elements in visual images leads to another. The former makes it possible to use 'first in the temporal sequence' to convey a significance different to that of 'last in the temporal sequence' so that the event which is mentioned first might carry the meaning 'cause of the event which follows' (e.g. John came into the room, and Mary left). The latter makes it possible to use 'central in a spatial composition' to convey a significance different to that of 'on the margin of the spatial composition' so that the element which is in the centre might carry the meaning 'focus of the composition', while marginal elements may be interpreted as 'context for the focal element'. The same principles apply to all modes.

Where we might seem to have borrowed from linguistics is in the taking over from Michael Halliday's functional linguistics of his ideas of the essential functions which any full communicational system must meet. For him these are three: that such a system must be able to represent and communicate states of affairs in the world (who or what is involved in what processes or relations, e.g. *'the farmer* **sold** *the bag of wheat', 'the bag of wheat* **is** *heavy'*), which Halliday calls the *ideational function*; that it must be able to represent and communicate the social/affective relations between the participants in the act of communication (e.g. the expression of differences of power: *'Could* **you** *possibly* **close the door,** *please?'*), which he calls the *interpersonal function*; and that it must be able to represent and communicate the utterance as fitting into a context both of the other elements of the text and of the wider environment, and in doing so produce coherence (the linking to another speaker's utterance, and to the wider environment in which this utterance is located), for instance: 'Was *it* **Wednesday** you said *that you'd be coming?'*

We regard these, following Halliday (1985), as general requirements of any human communicational system. The fact that they were first articulated in relation to language does not therefore make them linguistic; rather, it shows their appearance in the modes of speech and of writing. Thus we ask 'How are these functions realized in this mode?'

What we have taken over from a theory of language is therefore not a description of language, but a description of human semiosis in its most general form, appearing in this instance in the mode of language as speech and as writing.

In our descriptions throughout this book we make a distinction between representation and communication. In reality the two are inseparable – representation is always communicated (even if only to oneself) – yet it seems important to us to keep them theoretically distinct: *representation* focuses on what the individual wishes to represent about the thing represented; *communication* focuses on how that is done in the environment of making that representation suitable for a specific other, a particular audience. This is what we term *rhetoric*. An example is the representation of a plant cell as a three-dimensional model (discussed in the following section). The student represents the nucleus with a piece of bath sponge because she imagines the nucleus as the brain of the cell, and the sponge *represents* precisely the sponginess and the absorbent powers of the brain. That she then colours it red is to make it appear salient for the beholder of the model, that is, focusing much more on its *communicative* aspect. Of course, the sponginess also communicates and the redness also represents, but the two aspects are differentially foregrounded.

Motivated signs

Semiotics takes the *sign* as its basic unit of meaning. The sign is a unit in which a form has been combined with a meaning or, put differently, a form has been chosen to be the carrier of a meaning. A red rose, for instance, has been chosen as the carrier of the meaning 'I love you'. The red rose has become a sign. While the red rose stood in the bucket in the street outside the florist shop with two dozen others it was not a sign, though it had the potential to become one. In the western European tradition of the twentieth and twenty-first centuries the assumption has been that the relation between the form and the meaning in the sign is an arbitrary one, that is, that any other form could have been chosen instead as the carrier for the intended meaning. But, as this last example suggests, that is not in fact a plausible assumption. There is a good reason why the red rose was selected by the culture even though it might have chosen many other flowers, or fruit, or stones, etc. In social semiotics, in contrast to the dominant view, the assumption is that the relation between form and meaning, signifier and signified, is never arbitrary, but that it is always motivated by the interests of the maker of the sign to find the best possible, the most plausible form for the expression of the meaning that (s)he wishes to express.

The assumption about the motivated character of the relation between form and meaning is crucial if one wishes to develop a theory of meaning in which individuals are real *makers* of meaning, and not merely instantiators of existing conventions. If we ask children in the science classroom to produce a three-dimensional model of a plant cell and we look at how they have chosen to represent their understanding of what a cell is in their model, it is important to have a theory which attributes intent to all aspects of their choices of representation. If a child chooses to represent the nucleus of the cell with a piece of bath sponge which she has coloured red, then on the basis of the theory of the motivated sign we must ask 'What was it that this child was attempting to represent by choosing a piece of sponge and what was she attempting to represent by (the act of dyeing it) red?' As it happens, our subsequent interviews with the child revealed quite explicit reasons. This student conceived of the nucleus as the 'nerve-centre', the brain of the cell, so sponginess indicated both the sponginess of the brain, but also its absorptive power; red, on the other hand, was chosen to make the nucleus appear prominent, salient, as befits the nucleus of a cell.

The second respect in which the motivated relation between signifier and signified is crucial is in its relation to our understanding of learning. We return to that later, but here we simply say that any attempt to theorize learning as an active process engaged in by the learner demands this particular conception of sign-making.

The sign is always only a partial representation of the object represented, since it represents the interest of the sign-maker at the point of making the sign, and the sign-maker's interest is always partial. In making the models of the plant cell, the children selected those elements and those characteristics of the elements which engaged and represented their interest at that point. In this they act no differently from the scientists who focus on that which they see as crucial to their project at a specific moment, or from advertisers who represent those aspects of the thing advertised which seem most salient for their purposes, for their interest.

Transformation and learning

The sign-maker uses existing materials to make a sign. These may be culturally 'unformed' material things (the pebble that acts as the signifier for 'nucleus' in another three-dimensional model of the plant cell); already made and shaped by the culture and with meanings accruing from their uses in it (the clingfilm used as the membrane for the plant cell model); or the material of prior semiotic constructions (words, syntactic forms, generic forms of diagrams, and so on). Yet in the making of signs these materials are transformed: the clingfilm becomes a cell membrane, the pebble becomes the nucleus, the James Bond spy thriller genre becomes the signifier for the report on the journey of the red blood cell, and so on.

The existing culturally laden material is again changed in the process of becoming the best possible, the most plausible, the most apt signifier for the new signified. This is, of course, the process of *analogy* in which an aspect of the thing to be represented is materially expressed in the apt signifier in the production of a metaphor.

In our approach, every sign is the production of a new metaphor brought about through the process of analogy. Hence, in our approach there is no mere sign-*use*; there is therefore no re-use of already existing metaphors. There is the constant transformation of existing signifier resources (and existing metaphors then become part of this signifier resource), and the constant making of new metaphors. The process is guided by the *interest* of the individual sign-maker, so that both the individual's perception of the social world and the expression of their affective state enter into the new sign as the expression of their interest. This is so whether the sign is outwardly made, whether in speaking or in the making of a model, or made 'inwardly', in the process of 'taking in' the impressions of the external world, in apperception generally, or in reading. The process of reading is the internal process of new sign-making, in which the sign-components of texts are treated as signifiers to which signifieds need to be attached on the basis of the interest of the reader.

This transformative process constantly reshapes the culturally available resources of representation; and through this the historical changes in representational resources such as language-as-speech come about. Simultaneously, the sign-maker remakes the resources of representation available, thereby remaking their potential for self-representation, and their conceptual, cognitive, affective 'inner' world. This, we believe, is the process which we describe as 'learning', though it is also the process whereby the individual constantly remakes her or himself.

In a multimodal conception this process occurs through the multiplicity of modes involved and, given the materiality of the modes, it happens via the involvement of the various senses which are engaged in the 'taking in', the apperception of the external, semiotically shaped world. What is taken in in one mode interacts with what is taken in in other modes via other senses and thus an image perceived and transformed may reappear as a part of a verbal text (as we show in later chapters), and a verbally received and transformed sign may reappear as an 'external' representation in image form, and so on.

Design and innovation

The monomodal world (apart from always being a misperception of the communicational situation) had its clear stance on representation: here was a code, language, fully capable of expressing all articulate thought. But did the individual who wished to represent have full mastery of this code? If so, a speaker would encode meanings fully and adequately, and a hearer or reader who was similarly competent would be able to decode the message perfectly. This model has been subjected to sustained critique since the late 1960s, with Roland Barthes' *The Death of the Author* (1968) marking the beginning of that reassessment.

This view is not tenable in the multimodal world both for reasons we have already given (meaning is sign-making and therefore transformative rather than conservative sign-use) and because in the multimodal world meaning is always made using a multiplicity of modes, so that the question of *choice of mode* arises immediately. This involves the sign-maker in *design* decisions: 'Which mode, given this audience, will be best for representing and communicating that which I wish to communicate?' The interest of the sign-maker is engaged in two ways: in terms of the *design of representation*, and in terms of the *design of the message for communication*. Of course the question of the functional specialization of modes enters here: is the temporal logic of speech more apt than the spatial logic of image? But equally, the cultural histories of modes in a particular culture enter into consideration: certain modes have been traditionally used for certain purposes, modes have specific cultural valuations, etc.

With *design*, the agency of the individual as designer/sign-maker has become central: *interest* is that which finds its realization in the design, modulated of course by an awareness of the audience and the constraints which its expectations bring. Agency is present in the transformative aspect of sign-making and in the designing of the message for communication. In our explorations of learning and teaching in classrooms, students and teachers are agentive (under differing conditions of course, with differing powers, and with differing interests) and represent and communicate on the basis of their interests.

This approach has innovation at its centre. Innovation is the normal condition of all human meaning-making. An education system which denies what are to us the palpable facts of human semiosis sacrifices the central resource of its society.

Language

Language is not absent from our discussion, but nor is it central. It is present among all the other modes but foregrounded only when it *is* in the representational ensemble.

We have attempted by and large to avoid the term language, replacing it where possible with the couplet 'speech and writing'. Our reasons for this arise out of our theoretical position. It seems clear to us that speech and writing function as distinct semiotic modes as a result of their quite distinct materialities: the medium of sound versus the medium of graphic substance. We are aware of the intricate connection between the two modes, but we are equally aware of a distorting commonsense view which still treats writing as the process of making speech visible and permanent. Writing is more than that, and given the high status of writing in our cultures, this has led reciprocally to deep misunderstandings and disvaluations of speech.

Neither mode is served by this, nor is the culture in which such misunderstanding is active, nor the children who participate in an education system founded in large part on that skewed perception.

We have also attempted to stay away from the term language in as far as it points to a high abstraction, reification and generalization which obliterates the possibilities of considering the real difference in the structures and affordances of speech and writing, moves right away from the possibility of considering the material aspects of either speech or writing, and generally privileges mentalist conceptions of language over those which attempt to focus on its materiality and the consequences thereof.

We have been accused at times of having lost interest in language or writing, in favour of image. That is not the case. We think that the moment requires a new look at the place and the functions of language, and of writing in particular; not because of a lack of interest in language, but precisely the opposite. We feel that in order to newly and properly understand language we need to step outside it and take a satellite view of it. We hope by implication that our book says more about language, whether as speech or as writing, than do many other books which have language as their central focus.

The origins of this book

Most immediately this book arises out of an ESRC-funded research project, The Rhetorics of the Science Classroom: A Multimodal Approach (directed by Gunther Kress and Jon Ogborn, with researchers Carey Jewitt and Charalampos Tsatsarelis), conducted at the Institute of Education, University of London. That project followed on from two others, Explanation in the Science Classroom and Visual Communication in the Learning of Science. This book is thus the outcome of a gradually deepening sense of the complexities of the task of teaching science, an increasing awareness of the intricate orchestrations of resources that science teachers are constantly engaged in, and a wish to provide some means of clearer documentation and analysis of that task.

On the other hand, there was a developing theory of representation and communication based on a socially founded semiotics for which making meaning is the result of *work,* done by people in the contingencies of their social lives with all its complexity, who engage with the world in a multiplicity of sensual ways and who have affective dimensions to their lives which suffuse all those aspects we term cognition, learning, motivation, and so on. The first is the broad theoretical framework of social semiotics. The second is the growing theoretical framework of multimodality, the multiplicity of engagements with the world, a material and culturally socially shaped world (see Kress, 2000a; Kress and van Leeuwen, forthcoming).

The science classroom has turned out to be an excellent test-bed for these theoretical developments and has also posed challenges and problems which have forced us to continue to develop our theoretical framework in the course of our research, and to attempt to come up with solutions to problems of description: How can we represent in a sensible, readable form, the complexities of what goes on?

Hence this project became more than a description of complex practices, histories and institutions; it changed the way we came to think. Our own sense of the ancient and well-worked notion of rhetoric became clearer to us and a framework for dealing with units within a rhetorical approach was developed, as was a descriptive apparatus for handling multimodal communication. Our sense of the interrelations of the modes became clearer, as did our general understanding of human semiosis – how humans make meanings, represent and respond to these meanings, and rework the meanings of others. This is perhaps clearest in its effects on our conceptions of learning, and above all, on what we might best be able to use as evidence for documenting the processes of learning. We believe we have taken some modest steps in that direction.

1

Rhetorics of the science classroom: A multimodal approach

Introduction

This chapter focuses on the methodological issues of a multimodal approach to teaching and learning in the science classroom, and provides a theoretical and methodological frame for the reading of the book as a whole. This approach presents three main challenges to commonly held views on science education, and education in general. First, that the teaching and learning of science are purely linguistic accomplishments. Through attention to a variety of semiotic resources operating in the science classroom we demonstrate that each mode contributes to teaching and learning as *multimodal accomplishments* in specific ways. Second, that science education is not in need of rhetoric. Through detailed analysis of classroom interactions we show how students' views of the world are reshaped in the science classroom. Third, that learning is an acquisitive process in which students 'acquire' information directly from the teacher (or from textbooks, worksheets, etc.), which marginalizes the role of students in learning; or that it is a process in which the teacher facilitates the students' discovery of 'the facts', which marginalizes the role of the teacher. Learning, we suggest, needs to be seen as a dynamic process of transformative sign-making which actively involves both teacher and students.

The decision to focus on science education is not meant to suggest that science is essentially different from or more in need of rhetoric than other school-curriculum subjects. The decision was a pragmatic one. The regular use of action and image in the science classroom brings into immediate focus the issues raised in *multimodal communication*. The science classroom provides an environment where the shaping of students' views of the world is not always ready-made, 'off-the-cultural-shelf'; the shapings are often built within the environment of the classroom. Locating this study in the science classroom brings into sharp focus the need for an understanding of the semiotics of multimodal communication, because here the concrete material 'stuff' used in communicating the matter of science education cannot be ignored. The materials, chemicals, apparatus and models are all imbued with meaning and thus force attention onto the role of *action* in the learning process. Through a social semiotic analysis of the multimodal environment of the science classroom we hope to develop new understandings of learning in the science classroom and in education generally.

A social semiotic approach to multimodality

Three theoretical points inform our account of multimodal communication in the classroom. First, *media of communication* are shaped and organized by a culture into a range of meaning-making systems, *modes,* in order to articulate the meanings demanded by the practical, social requirements of different communities. The use of different modes leads to meanings being made differently. First, the meanings made are not always equally accessible to and understood by all readers. Second, the meanings made with language, whether as speech or as writing, are interwoven with the meanings made with other modes in the communicative context, and this interaction itself produces meaning. Third, the question of what is to be considered a *communicative mode* remains open. Systems of meaning-making resources are neither static nor stable, but fluid. Modes of communication develop in response to the communicative needs of society; new modes are created, and existing modes are transformed.

Halliday's social theory of communication (Halliday, 1985) provides the starting-point for our exploration of multimodal teaching and learning in the science classroom. Halliday argues that in verbal interactions with others we have at our disposal networks of meaning options (sets of semiotic alternatives), which are realized through the means of representation, themselves organized as systems of choices. The elements of the semantic system of language reflect three social functions of the utterance – representation, interaction, and message – and these are realized (in language) by the lexico-grammar. The all-important principle at the base of this model is that language is as it is because of the tasks it is asked by its users to perform. It is organized to function with respect to the social interests of its users and the demands made of it by them. With more emphasis on the agentive role of individuals in interaction, we might say that language is as it is because we constantly reshape it in the light of our interests at the moment of interaction.

Language-as-speech can thus be understood as the result of the working or 'shaping' by a culture (through the agency of its individual members) of a material (sound) into a cultural medium, and then further shaped as the mode of speech. Of course other cultural shapings of sound have led to other modes, music most prominently.

We suggest that, like language, visual images, gesture and action have also been developed through their social usage into articulated or partially articulated resources for representation into modes. We have extended Halliday's conception of language as a social semiotic device to suggest that each of these modes has been developed into articulated semiotic systems made up of networks of interlocking options (or alternatives). The alternatives that are selected within these networks of meaning can be seen as traces of the sign-maker's attempt to choose the most apt and plausible signifier for the expression of meaning in a given context. In this we see one expression of the sign-maker's *interest* (Kress, 1997). In short, we understand teaching and learning in the science classroom to be the material expression, the 'evidence', of the (cognitively and affectively) motivated choices of teachers and students from among the meaning-making resources available in a particular situation (here the science classroom) at a given moment.

In order to explore how each mode operating in the science classroom contributes to the processes of teaching and learning we draw on the notion of *grammar as a meaning-making resource* (Halliday, 1985) for encoding interpretations of experience and forms of social action. We use the term *grammar* to refer loosely to the structures of relations of elements in a specific mode, and between modes, which have become established over time rather than seeing grammar as a system of formal rules of correctness.

> It [grammar] is a means of representing patterns of experience. . . . It enables human beings to build a mental picture of reality, to make sense of their experience of what goes on around them and inside them. (Halliday, 1985:101)

This notion of grammar has been extended to encompass the mode of the visual:

> Just as grammars of language describe how words combine in clauses, sentences and texts, so our visual 'grammar' will describe the way in which depicted people, places and things combine in visual 'statements' of greater or lesser complexity and extension. (Kress and van Leeuwen, 1996:1)

We use grammar as a conceptual tool to explore how meanings are actualized through speech, writing, images and other aspects of the visual (including the body, movement and interaction with objects) in science classroom teaching and learning. In particular, we comment on how meanings are made through the intricate weaving together of meaning across and between these modes. Our starting-point was to explore how the potentials for meaning which are developed within each mode are used by the teacher to realize meanings in writing, in demonstration and through graphs. We did this by considering the *affordances* of each of the modes, that is, we asked the question 'What constraints and possibilities for making meaning are offered by each mode present for representation in the science classroom, and what use is made of them?' Our working assumption was that in the history of science teaching each mode has been worked (shaped) differently to realize meanings appropriate for these purposes. The question for us was, what potentials for meaning-making are available in each mode, and how are these potentials arranged ('structured') to make meaning in the science classroom? Our work was therefore oriented to the detailed description of speech, writing, gesture and action, and the visual, and the description of their interaction in communicational ensembles and in their use in this environment. The question was, how do they function as resources for meaning-making?

Halliday's *meaning-making principles,* what he calls the three meta-functions of language, informed our analysis of multimodal communication. Within this model all communication is understood to realize three kinds of meaning: to represent what is going on in the world (what Halliday calls *ideational meaning*); to bring about interactions and relations between people (*interpersonal meaning*); and to form communicatively meaningful whole entities, *texts* (*textual meaning*). The meaning of any text comes from the interplay between these three types of meaning. Each can be viewed as the result of selections from a range of possible meaning-features, and the action of selection represents the work which is required of students and teachers when producing or making sense of (i.e. reproducing internally) a text.

The set of features which comprise the *ideational meanings* of any semiotic mode concern who does what, with or to whom, and where. In language this articulates our experience of the world as one in which entities are involved in and related by processes which may be material ('boiling'), verbal ('reporting'), mental ('considering'), or relational ('being', 'having'). Hence this function deals with the interrelation of participants and circumstances in the representation of the world in such processes. The *interpersonal meanings* of any semiotic mode used in a communicative act function to establish, maintain and specify the relationships between members of societies or groups through expression of the social relations which are felt in the members' environment. These may refer to expressions of the inextricable interrelations of power and knowledge. The *textual meanings,* realized through the textual resources of a mode, 'breathe relevance into the other two' (Halliday, 1985: xiii). They organize the text as a coherent message relevant to the situation, producing (in a well-formed text) a coherent account of the world. Although ideational, interpersonal and textual meanings are distinct, they are always integrated in communication and all three are in simultaneous operation.

Linguistic approaches to the meaning of classroom interaction see meaning as residing in the interplay between the ideational, interpersonal and textual features of writing or speech (even if in different theories it is not necessarily expressed in these terms). From a multimodal perspective, the approach involves attending to the interplay between these three types of meanings in and across each of the modes in use, which multiplies the complexity of meaning. Each mode of communication interacts with and contributes to the other. At times the meanings realized in two modes may be equivalent, often they are complementary, sometimes one repeats information presented in the other. Additionally, each may refer to quite different aspects of meaning, or the two may be contradictory (Kress, 1994; Lemke, 1998). In short, modes produce meaning in themselves and through their intersection or interaction with each other. Our research suggests that in multimodal communication the different modes take on specialized tasks, broadly along the lines of their inherent affordances, and the specialized meaning resources in one mode combine with those of another to produce more complex, modulated meanings. Thus communication in the science classroom is always more than a sequential shift from one mode to another.

From our data we can demonstrate that attention to one mode alone fails to capture the meaning of a communicative event; not just that it fails to capture all the meaning, but that it fails to capture *the* meaning. Meaning resides in the combined effects of the orchestration of the modes by the producer and by the reproducer, in the interaction between what is said, what is shown, the posture adopted, the movements made, and the position of the speaker and the audience relative to each other in the interaction.

The teacher's selection of communicative modes (the way in which something is communicated) combined with the reciprocal *actions* on the part of the students is, for us, the process of creating meaning (We take that to be a general statement about all communication).

In other words, teachers' and students' selection of modes in the science classroom can be understood as one aspect of their active engagement in the sign-making process. We now move on to briefly clarify some of the ideas and terms involved in multimodal analysis.

A language of description

Medium and mode

We use *medium* (and the plural *media*) to refer to the material substance which is worked on or shaped over time by culture into an organized, regular, socially specific means of representation, i.e. a meaning-making resource or a *mode*. For instance, the medium of sound has been worked into the mode of language-as-speech and of music. The medium of light has been shaped through a range of technologies into photography and (contemporary) art. The movement of the body in time and space has been articulated into a variety of modes to express a range of meanings. Classical ballet or Indian dance, for example, use the movement of bodies in space and time to tell narratives, but like all systems of meaning (including language) these narratives are not available to all readers. Gesture, a species of action, has become a mode which generally accompanies speech. However, gesture has also been fully articulated into mode, for example in the sign languages of the communities of the hearing and speech impaired, and in sign systems such as semaphore. Different periods in time have witnessed the articulation of various media into fully articulated communicational modes, and the transformation of elements of the modes themselves (e.g. perspective in the mode of visual image) in ways which offer new potentials for meaning-making. In the light of this, we were particularly interested to explore how particular modes had evolved in the context of the science classroom.

Materiality

The inherent characteristics of the material used by a culture for making meanings, with and out of which it shapes the different media, has its effects on what meanings can be made: the matter of *affordances* mentioned above. For instance, the temporal/sequential characteristics of human sound make certain things easily possible and impede certain others that are readily possible in the spatial/ simultaneous medium of graphic representation. This leads us to say that each meaning-making system – *mode* – provides different communicative potentials. In other words, each mode is culturally shaped around the constraints and affordances of its medium – its *materiality*. The materiality of speech is sequences of sounds in time (i.e. air pressure variations and their productive and receptive effects in the body) which produce a specific physical sensation. In contrast, the materiality of visual communication can be thought of as spatial, with units of meaning that are experienced simultaneously rather than in sequence, through light as graphic substance. The materiality of gesture and action is more complex than either the linguistic or the visual since it places meaning-making into three dimensions – temporality (movement) in sequence, spatial (position) and displacement in (three-dimensional) space. The meaning-making possibilities and limitations provided by the materiality of each mode, and the degree to which a mode has been developed within a given culture and social contexts, raise the issue of *representational* and *communicational specialization* of the modes.

The materiality of the manner of transmission is also a part of the process of meaning-making. We use *channel* and *means of dissemination* to refer to these aspects of multimodal communication. By channel we mean both the physiological channel (e.g. via the ear, eye or touch) and the technological channel (being in a concert hall as opposed to listening to the radio at home, or listening to a digital CD of the same performance), and both shape the way in which meanings are communicated. The *means of dissemination* as much as the agent of dissemination (adult/child, man/woman, violin/ saxophone) are further factors which impact upon the realization of particular meanings.

Functional specialization

Alongside others (e.g. Lemke, 1998) we argue that science education (and science) no longer relies on verbal language alone (particularly language-as-writing) in its efforts to describe the material interactions of people with the natural world. Implicit in this argument is the assertion that visual, actional and linguistic modes of communication have been refined through their social usage to make meaning in different ways and to produce different meaning-making potentials – what we refer to as *functional specialization* or *functional specialisms.* That is, there are some things that some modes have been developed to do better than others. The meaning-making potentials of the resources of the visual, actional and linguistic modes each perform a special and differently significant role. In communication the choices made from each of these sets of potentials are rhetorically organized to provide an integrated multimodal whole. These potentials are the result of the combined effects of the inherent attributes of the materials and of their transformation over very long stretches of history, in particular, cultures into modes. Whether the consequences of the social usages of modes, and the status this has afforded a particular set of them, or the inherent characteristics are the more significant at a particular point in the history of a culture is the subject of a very different study.

In this way, the selection of modes by the teacher can be viewed as a part of the rhetorical process. Each mode offers the rhetor (teacher *or* student in this case) different ways of representing the world as 'knowledge'. The process of organizing these modes into a communicative event involves consideration of what is to be communicated, and how this can best be done given the functional specialisms of each mode available within the science classroom, the interests of the communicator, and her or his (constantly adjusting) sense of the audience. In short, the mode of communication enters potently into the shaping of meaning, both in relation to knowledge ('Is image the best mode to represent the characteristic of this knowledge?') and in relation to audience ('Is a photo the best way to capture the attention of my class at this moment?').

One difficulty with our analytical approach to classroom communication as a multimodal event is that it makes the most prosaic classroom interactions appear enormously complex. The same thing occurs when linguists undertake a detailed analysis of talk in the classroom: language appears as the product of a myriad of complex social decisions, something which does not reflect the ease with which the majority of people engage in the everyday task of speaking.

There is a disjuncture between the speaker's conscious engagement with the task and the linguistic analytical procedures. Nonetheless speakers are engaged in a complex task. This disjuncture becomes more insistent when communication in the classroom is looked at as a multimodal event. A multimodal approach can turn what goes on in the classroom into an implausibly intricate and complex event which seems beyond the capabilities of any human brain to manage. However, we are not suggesting that the multimodal orchestration involved in communication is always consciously available to teachers and students. Perhaps it is useful here to make a distinction between what we could call the 'everyday communicational modes' and the 'prepared media' in the science classroom (boards, slides, OHPs, demonstrations and so on), that is, the routines which teachers have developed in order to cope with the complexity of the task. In the former the teacher/student may be less conscious of the resources they are using to shape meaning and the shifts between them; in the latter, conscious attention is given to making multimodality work.

The question of the plausibility of the theoretical framework is important. At this point we can say three things:

(i)   the complexity of even the simplest task cannot be overstated;

(ii) the question of 'routines' of all kinds, in all communication and in all modes, offers one way of thinking about plausible simplification (the routines of a squash player in playing a shot no less than the routines involved in the most ordinary-seeming social interaction); and

(iii) these are questions occupying many disciplines at the moment, and we can do no more than acknowledge the difficulties at this point.

Rhetorics of the science classroom

Our interest in the rhetorics of the science classroom developed from earlier work on explanation in the science classroom (Ogborn *et al.*, 1996). In this book we show that explanation (as a certain kind of generic framing) is one of many rhetorical strategies employed by science teachers to shape knowledge in the domain of science education. This shaping is founded, primarily, on the construction of entities and the relationships between them in order to shape students' views of the world in particular ways. For example, the use of scientific equipment to enable students to see entities which are usually invisible to them (such as microbes, cells or bacteria) or to demonstrate abstract concepts (such as energy) in concrete ways. Knowledge may also be shaped by the rhetorical transformation of everyday entities into scientific entities (e.g. the onion used in an experiment to display the nature of plant cells temporally ceases to be thought of as food, and instead becomes a collection of cells for the time of the investigation), or the linking of seemingly disparate things (such as parts of the body being linked to present the body as a system, or the rethinking of the earth as a part of the universe).

We suggest that the shaping of knowledge in this way is achieved by rhetorical means; the shapes of knowledge are realized by rhetorical framings which are identifiable by specific, identifiable textual shifts and combinations. As such we view rhetorical frames as socially constructed ways of realizing the otherwise abstract shaping of knowledge. The rhetorical frames are themselves realizations of specific epistemologies (which we at times describe as ideological structures) which arise from and are produced by the social conditions in which they become relevant, the science classroom in our case. For example, the rhetorics of the science classroom arise from the pedagogic requirement to create *difference* (see Ogborn *et al.,* 1996) and the resultant need for explanations, to place science outside of the social domain, and to provide new tools for thinking with.

We have briefly argued against the notion that science education stands outside of rhetoric which is a view that has dominated the general approach to science education over the past two decades. Science education has been based on the premise that it is nature, not teachers, which persuades students of scientific truths because the facts speak for themselves. Within this approach students simply receive science on the grounds of belief while the teacher's role is to facilitate the students' experience of natural phenomena so that they may learn. In short, science teaching simply lets students see how it is for themselves. In this way hearing and seeing have come to be synonymous with learning. In our view, this approach has failed to provide an adequate account of the process of meaning-making (which, as we will argue, is 'learning' from another perspective) in the science classroom, particularly in relation to the role of teachers in learning.

This book attempts to highlight the complex ways in which semiotic resources are rhetorically orchestrated in the science classroom, and the central role of the teacher in this and in the process of learning. At the same time the book asserts the active role of students in the processes of learning and teaching both because as the teacher's audience students have their impact on teaching as rhetoric and because of their own transformative role in their shaping of meaning. The book shows how students' views of the world are shaped through the active communicative choices of modes and contents (whether consciously or unconsciously), selections from the rich environment of the classroom, and the transformations which they and teachers make constantly in the classroom. Although we see the teacher as central to this process, we envisage this rhetorical shaping as a dialogic process in which teachers (and the school) provide the ideological/rhetorical frame within which students are active participants in a dynamic process. In this context, it is notable that we do not see the experiences, interests, and knowledge that students bring to the process of learning as the process of learning itself; rather we see these as key materials which are available for and which inform learning.

Our choice of 'rhetorics' as a term is a shorthand way of encapsulating the approach outlined above. The use of this term has, perhaps predictably, caused us some problems. The historical associations of rhetoric and the vagueness of the term have at times overshadowed its usefulness. The notion of a stable semiotic foundation beneath the decorative surface of rhetoric, which is as implicit in classical notions of rhetoric as in contemporary commonsense, has been particularly problematic. Classical definitions of *rhetoric* as the skill of an orator in persuading an audience carry with them a notion of rhetoric as a set of linguistic devices in relation to particular functions. In contrast, we view semiotic systems as unstable and undergoing constant transformation through the interests of social actors engaged in interaction with others. From a social semiotic viewpoint there is no plain, stable language on which to build and which to adorn: all language use is always 'interested', and socially engaged. Nonetheless, the use of the term rhetorics has been useful in positioning our analysis outside of the anti-rhetorical view of science education, and has served to emphasize the central role of the teacher in teaching and learning, in making decisions and choices, rather than as a neutral observer of students' engagement with 'the facts'. The term rhetoric highlights that in attempting to shape students' conceptions of the world, teachers are acting rhetorically: they present a plausible, integral and coherent account of the world through the orchestration of a range of communicational means.

In our reappropriation of rhetoric we use the term to refer to the material semiotic realization of intentions or purposes of interaction in ways which effect students' views of the world. This book sets out to document some of the key ways in which students are brought, through their engagement with education, to see the world in different ways and to reorganize their existing views into new frameworks. It also provides detailed analyses of how teachers harness different modes and means in an attempt to persuade students to view an aspect of the world in a particular way.

Rhetorical framing of teaching and learning

We analysed interaction in the classroom with two questions in mind: (i) How are meanings realized at the level of mode? (as discussed in the previous section); and (ii) How is the science classroom rhetorically organized? In this way our analysis explored both the semiotic features and structures of communication in the science classroom, and its broader rhetorical aspects. We view rhetoric and social semiotics as compatible paradigms which offer different and complementary perspectives on communication. The in-depth semiotic description of meaning-making in the science classroom provides a focus on the characteristics of the stuff of which meaning is made. A rhetorical approach places a broader focus on the pedagogic role of the teacher. This shifts the focus between the social reasons for the shaping of the 'stuff' in modes, and the rhetorical (pedagogical) strategies and themes through which the 'stuff' is shaped as a coherent account of the world, offers an account of the overall organization of the interaction, and emphasizes the interests of both teachers and students. Thus we have approached interaction from two perspectives, and through the iterative analysis of each we have attempted to say something about the relationship between them (between the shaping of the 'stuff' and the shaping of the larger frames in which it is communicated) and the potentials for transformative learning. We suggest that this relationship is dialectical: the modes of communication operating in the classroom are the means through which rhetoric is realized, while at the same time the rhetoric gives a particular shape to the modes of communication, realizing them as elements of social action.

We see the task of shaping knowledge in the science classroom as happening over time and motivated by the interests, experiences and values of teachers, school policy, national policy and legislation. We suggest that teachers' rhetorical intentions motivate the 'rhetorical framing' of lessons which reflects one expression of the teacher's rhetorical intentions. The rhetorical frame is realized by a textual form of rhetoric, that is, it is identifiable by shifts in textualization – socially constructed ways of realizing the shapes of knowledge drawing on specific epistemologies.

We draw on the notion of *frame* in our analysis of the rhetorics of the science classroom. Frames both classify activities and interpret them, while serving to locate, perceive, identify and label the everyday. In our analysis of multimodal communication we use frame as an analytical tool, to draw attention to the ways in which teachers and students negotiate and structure the meaning of experience through the use of rhetorical frames. This is the rhetorical organization of the pedagogic experience. Bateson argues that actions which people engage in do not always denote 'what those actions for which they stand would denote' (Bateson, 1987: 180); that is 'the frame' indicates what people should attend to; it is a part of the premises of communication. The picture frame, for example, instructs the viewer not to use the same sort of thinking in interpreting a picture that she or he might use in interpreting the wallpaper. In other words, we can view frame as a form of instruction to aid understanding of the meaning-making process. Our conception of frame is further informed by

Goffman's (1974) frame analysis to address the experimental modes and devices available to us for making sense out of events (e.g. ritual, drama and games), that is devices which illuminate frameworks of social interaction (Goffman, 1974; Crook and Taylor, 1980).

A teacher's movement in the classroom, interaction with resources and communicative actions all serve to realize the student's relationship with knowledge: the rhetorics of the science classroom. In a lesson on particles with Year 9 students, the teacher's movement from the front to the back of the classroom as she talked was one element which marked the boundary between rhetorical frames. In addition to this gross shift in position, the rhetorical reframing of the lesson was marked by the teacher shifting attention from her body as the canvas for a pantomimic demonstration of states of matter (gas, liquid and solid) to a scientific model of particles in each of these states of matter (i.e. a change in the means of the explanation), the change in the teacher's height-position in the classroom as she moved from the floor onto the raised podium at the front of the classroom, a significant change in her posture as she placed and held her hand on her hip, and the teacher's transition from an exploratory style of speech to the use of analogy. All of these elements shaped the authoritative rhetoric of the scientific knowledge presented.

Our analysis of the science classroom shows that rhetorical framing of this kind can occur at different structural/organizational levels – a series of lessons, individual lessons, and/or sections of lessons. This framing is achieved through particular configurations of modes and means in the classroom. Shifts in the configuration of these elements result in different and distinct rhetorical frames, each of which impacts on the teacher–student relationship and their relationships to science and learning.

In a lesson on energy involving an investigation of what makes a good fuel, there was a striking contrast between the actions of the students in the first and second trial of the investigation. We suggest that this contrast can be read as signifying a change in the students' interests and motivation, a shift in their involvement in the investigation, and ultimately as the dissolving of the rhetorical frame of the investigation.

During the first trial of the investigation the students stood still and upright as a group around the table, their gaze fixed on the equipment, in particular the clock, the boiling tube and the thermometer. Their talk focused on the process and collection of results and at the end of each phase of the trial the equipment was washed, cooled and set up in the same way. During the second trial the group was more disparate, one or two students gathered around the experiment then wandered away, at one point no one was present while the metafuel burned and boiled the water. The group had fragmented. Student body posture was casual and they gesticulated, moved around and paid poor attention to the setting up of the equipment (e.g. they used a test tube instead of a boiling tube, did not change the water in the test tube after each phase, put the thermometer in place only as the water started to boil, and rather than waiting for the metafuel to stop burning, one student blew it out).

We suggest that the rhetorical framing of the experiment – 'the scientific procedures for establishing things' – dissolved in the second trial as a result of the teacher's lack of framing of the task via verbal instructions and visually on the worksheet (which made no written or visual reference to the layout of the table or to repeating the trial). The students' actions were no longer entirely motivated by the concerns of the science classroom. Their own interests mediated their actions and in so doing they transformed the rhetorical frame of the investigation so as to reframe their actions within their systems of relevance of the everyday.

Through intensive viewing of the video data generated by the project and the application of the concept of frame described above, we classified the data into analytical units of *rhetorical frame*. This enabled us to manage the data analytically and to develop a descriptive language of rhetorical framing. In this descriptive language we focused on what the rhetorical frames were typically used for in the context of teaching science (their functions), rather than on the traditional categories of rhetoric (e.g. analogy) which focus more on the formal relations and processes of elements in a text with each other and with their environment We found that rhetorical frames were typically combined with a number of broad epistemological functions. These gave us broad categories (of rhetorical frame combined with rhetorical function) which (i) provided us with a set of criteria for the selection of case-study examples; (ii) enabled us to explore how modes realize rhetorical frames in specific ways (*functional specialism*); and (iii) illustrated ways in which rhetorical frames and modes are orchestrated (as a series of units) to shape students' views of the world.

To generalize, the rhetorical framing of the lessons we observed can to some extent be described as an attempt to unsettle or overthrow students' notions of reality. We classified the various realizations of this process and show them in Table 1.1 below. Each of the general epistemological functions was textualized in particular ways. In Table 1.1 we offer some instances of these specific textualizations and identify some key principles for the relationship between rhetorical frame and textualization of epistemological function.

The examples given here do not exhaust all the types. Other combinations of rhetorical frame and epistemological function that we found were *generalization* (and its textualizations as 'rubbing out difference', 'seeing similarities and spotting differences'); *classification* (and its textualizations as analogical processes); *cause and effect* (and its textualizations); *logical relations* (and its textualizations of the kind 'if X is true then Y is/is not true').

The book provides detailed exploration of the combination of different communicational modes to realize the rhetorical intentions of both teachers and students across an individual lesson and a series of lessons. In this way we provide a snapshot of how teachers work in realizing their pedagogic intentions through an ensemble of different modes. The book describes the rhetorical work of the classroom at a macro- and a micro-level. Through an iterative process it uses detailed analysis of and hypotheses on multimodal communication to build up an account of how the shaping of students' views of the world occurs in the science classroom. We do not see this as a necessarily conscious process. The realization of the teachers' intentions cannot be separated from the semiotic tools available to them in the classroom or the audience of students whose actions play a significant role in this. We view the relationship between mode, frame, and interest of teachers and students as dynamic and as reciprocally interacting.

Table 1.1 Rhetorical function and textual realization

Rhetorical function	Instances of textual realization
Ontology of the everyday	You can see this in your everyday life
	You've experienced its effect
	You've seen the evidence
See in a new way	Making the usually invisible visible (microscope)
	Reconstituting phenomena (for instance, by shifting attention/ focus (e.g. onion cells)
	Renaming of phenomena
Constructing knowledge as given fact	Through description
	Presentation of fact through pedagogic means (book)
	Through analogy
	Through classification
	Through empirical evidence and measurement
Authority of science/ teacher	I have the knowledge
	See it my way
	Think about it this way: think like the scientists
	Write about it this way: write it like the scientists
Historical pedigree	Scientific theory
	Historical material evidence (e.g. the world has a history)
Procedures for establishing knowledge	Observe and record
	Time and measure
	Fairness and repetition
	Objectivity: separation of action and thought

(Continued)

Table 1.1 (Continued)

Rhetorical function	Instances of textual realization
'Discovery'	Now you tell me
	Let's build on what you know
	Let's take this apart/build this together
	Write it in your own words
Reconstituting subjectivity	Reconstituting students' experiences (e.g. stars)
	Reconstituting students' identity (e.g. learner, expert, young scientist)

Rhetorical orchestration of meaning

The analysis in terms of rhetorical frames was applied to lessons to produce a map of the shifts in rhetoric across the lesson and series of lessons so as to reveal their *rhetorical architecture.* Mapping the rhetorical frames in this way enabled us (i) to describe instances of how rhetoric is constructed during a lesson and series of lessons and show the cumulative effect of rhetorical framing; and (ii) to explore how teachers and students differ in their organization of rhetorical frames, that is, in the *rhetorical architectures* of different classrooms, and how these realize different (rhetorical) meanings and effects.

As well as giving attention to how each mode makes meaning by itself, our aim was to identify the ways in which different modes of communication contribute to the rhetorical *orchestration of meaning* in the science classroom. We wish to be able to describe how teachers use image, action, manipulation of objects, speech, and so on to construct the entities of the science classroom, and how they realize other rhetorical functions in science lessons. From our analysis it is clear that each mode plays a distinct and different role in the realization of these rhetorical functions (as in our example of the visualization of the entity 'blood'). All the modes are jointly orchestrated across a lesson and across a series of lessons in order to build up meaning over time. In this way, we see meaning as emerging from a process of interaction, contrast and conjunction of the modes. Meaning is not a matter of each mode making discrete meanings within its particular realm of potentials, rather meaning emerges from the interweaving between and across modes within a multimodal system.

In our analyses of the orchestration of meaning across and between modes it became apparent that in the ensemble of co-present modes, there was a relation which we describe as *foregrounding* (that which is made salient or emphasized) or *backgrounding* (that which is not made salient or emphasized). It was not the case that all the modes were used equally and had the same communicational function. When teachers and students communicate they may draw attention to content or to a particular mode by making it prominent (by expanding or extending it) or they may do the opposite by backgrounding it or absenting it for stretches. In the case of visual communication an aspect of the mode may be foregrounded through exaggeration. In the example discussed in the next chapter colour is exaggerated to indicate the distinctness of each of the organs and the changes undergone by blood in its journey around the body. Alternatively, this feature of *grounding* can draw attention to a specific meaning across the modes within the communicative event as a whole. For example, as the lesson discussed in this chapter begins, the teacher takes the register. At this point each mode realizes the same interpersonal meaning of 'quiet control' through the physical stillness of his body, the monotone pitch of his voice as he reads out each name, and the blank whiteboard behind him. Here the communicational function of all the modes in play is kept equal: none is foregrounded, none is backgrounded.

Grounding is a subtle and effective device for the making and the orchestration of meaning. For instance, a specific mode may be foregrounded through an excess (or absence) of the *expected* use of a mode in the classroom. Of course one needs to be aware that at times it is the researcher who foregrounds aspects of meaning-making, for example in Chapter 3 our analysis foregrounds action in the multi-modal context of the science classroom in order to explore it as a meaning-making system. Foregrounding in analysis can be seen as a way of making salient aspects of what is going on. In contrast, backgrounding in the analysis can make something less salient. In this way, although the elements in play in a lesson may remain the same throughout, there is a shift in analytical emphasis on them.

Grounding is also available to the teacher to vary what is brought to the attention of the students. The process of moving between modes can serve to realize different meanings. When something is backgrounded for that moment it is not the object of attention. It is presented as unproblematic and becomes a given. Foregrounding and backgrounding can therefore be used in a shift across different modes to make meanings of this kind.

A multimodal approach draws attention to the communicative work teachers and students are engaged in to provide a new way of talking, and a new sense of what is going on both in classrooms and in communication more generally.

Rethinking learning

Viewing the science classroom as a multimodal environment has a number of implications for thinking about learning. A central implication is the relationship between mode and 'thinking'. If, as we have argued in this book and elsewhere (e.g. Kress *et al.*, 1998), different modes enable different representational work to be done – that is, that information and meaning have a very distinct shape in the different modes and permit different meanings to be conveyed – then it follows that each mode must also require different 'cognitive work' in order to be understood. In Chapter 2 we focus on what it means to learn in the multimodal environment of the science classroom. We approach students' texts[1] (and the decisions students engaged with in producing them) as providing a way into understanding the learning potential of multimodal communication in teaching approaches. Students' texts, we suggest, can be seen as an expression of how students engaged with knowledge in

---

[1] Here text relates to communication and describes the material realization (the visual and linguistic resources used) of the entity message in the act of communication. The term message is oriented towards the meaning to be communicated; the term text is oriented towards the material form of the message.

the classroom and so they constitute a singularly potent form of evidence of learning. We have argued that visual and actional forms of representation enable the expression of kinds of meaning which are difficult or impossible to make in language as speech or as writing. That is, that the modes provide different views of the world and therefore different potentials for learning. In this we have not yet considered the distinct physiological and psychological routes of information to the brain, or the effects of this on the possibilities for thinking and learning.

We explore how students use the resources made available to them by the teacher in the classroom and from other sources (e.g. from other lessons, as well as from outside the school: from television or students' own experiences and interests of the most diverse kinds) in order to construct meanings, produce their own rhetorically shaped versions of entities and concepts, and present themselves as 'learners of science'. For us, learning is the perpetually transformative action of sign-making through which students are involved in the active 'remaking' of teachers' (and others') signs according to the context of the lesson, and the different interests of the teacher and students.

Learning as a process of sign-making

Social semiotics informs our understanding of the process of learning as *a dynamic process of sign-making*. We view the situated communicative actions of the teacher as the semiotic material which contributes to the resources for and imposes some constraints on students' production of texts in the science classroom. We treat the students' texts as semiotic objects (signs) mediating their responses to the materials and the communicative actions made available in the classroom, and expressive of their interests. They thus represent one kind of evidence of what their thinking may have been like. For us, meaning-making is a motivated activity, in which the interest of the sign-maker (in this case the teacher and the students) is expressed through his or her selection of apt and plausible signifiers for the expression of their meanings in signs of their own new making in a given context (Kress, 1997). We are interested in how students transform these materials (both the structural and the content aspects of a teacher's communication) through the selection and the adaptation of elements presented, and the introduction of new elements. From a different perspective, this can be seen as the process of learning. We think that the best way to produce evidence for the cognitive processes of students' learning is to focus on the immediate outcome of this process in the form of texts of all kinds. This means that students' texts can be analysed as the consequences of their representational choices in terms of modes, elements and arrangements.

To clearly outline the process as we see it: we believe that 'acquisition' is an inappropriate metaphor to describe the processes of learning: it implies a stable system which is statically acquired by an individual. Instead we see learning as one of a series of processes of transformation. In apperception an individual makes selections from the world in focus, guided by her or his interest (which includes, of course, a sense of the social environment in which this happens). The apperceived world has its structure, which is not obvious, but is still the object of an interpretative/transformative activity by the individual again in the light of her or his interest, itself an effect of the already existing structures and dispositions of the individual. That is, the existing 'mental' disposition of the individual provides a kind of template for the transformation of the external structures in their apperception. In this way a new sign is produced 'inwardly': formed as a result of the (resistances of) the external structure, and the transformation of that in the light of the demands of the existing 'inner' structures. In re-presentation, a new, transformed inner configuration is the basis on which the new, outwardly made sign (in a combination of writing, gesture, image and speech) is made in the light of the individual's interest at that moment, which includes an assessment of the external environment in which this message/sign as communication is shaped. Consequently, sign-making is always transformative, always the making of a new sign, always changing both the shape of the resources and the disposition of the individual human subject.

Previous educational research has focused primarily on linguistic resources (talk, reading and writing), reflecting the dominant view of learning as primarily a linguistic accomplishment. By contrast we explore the full repertoire of meaning-making resources which students and teachers bring to the classroom. In our analyses we attempt to uncover how these are organized to make meaning in a multimodal approach to classroom interaction. Extending our view of communication to include other modes of meaning-making highlights the need to understand the ways in which these modes express social meanings. A multimodal social semiotic approach to students' texts opens the way to see the differences between them (and between those of the teacher's resources) not as markers of error, (lack of) understanding, or individual aesthetic (whether expressed through visual or other material/sensory means) but as a serious expression of different interests: as a transformation of the teachers' signs, together with materials drawn from the widest sources, made in a wide range of modes and materials, into new signs.

However, approaching learning as a dynamic process of sign-making reopens the question of why students' texts do vary. Nowadays it is less usual for educational practitioners and researchers to view the learning process as the transmission of knowledge from teacher to student. Despite this, the response to differences between students' texts is still seen as an indication of a student's failure to read (or reproduce) the stable messages encoded in teachers' communications correctly. By contrast, a social semiotic multimodal approach suggests that variation between students' texts is an expression of their different interests. That is, students' texts can be read as transformative of the original resources, as their shaping of meaning in what is for them the most apt and plausible way given the resources available to them in a specific context.

The physical characteristics of students' texts in the classroom have rarely been attended to as a serious issue within educational research. Where attention to the physical characteristics of texts has been given, it has provided a link between the study of texts and the study of practices, giving insight into children's literacy practices (Ormerod and Ivanic, 1999). The visual and linguistic resources which students draw on to make meaning in the science classroom can be viewed as their cultural working of a medium. As we have argued earlier, communicative media are worked and shaped over time into regular forms of representations, for instance as a grammar.

In this way they become the material (signifier) for the stuff of naming (sign). The meanings of students' texts are bound up with the choices which they make from a range of meaning-making systems, a variety of available materials, and the decisions they make in combining these. Students are constantly engaged in complex decisions when selecting how to represent something.

Multimodal analysis of the science classroom

In this section we offer a detailed account of the processes of data collection, transcription and analysis within the multimodal context of the science classroom.

Data collection

The data on which this study and many of our conclusions are based were collected from four secondary schools in London: a girls' comprehensive school, a community technical college, and two mixed comprehensive schools. The research demanded a strong commitment from each school in terms of organization, time and extended access to the classroom; the students and the schools were recruited via existing contacts with the heads of science. Through purposive selection of schools willing to participate we ensured that the project focused on schools with a range of academic achievements.

We collected a variety of data on a series of science lessons in each school, each with a different year group. The series of lessons we observed and video recorded focused on:

- Germs, diseases, lifestyle, and the immune system (with Year 7)

- Staying Alive: the organs and the blood (with Year 8)

- Energy, fuels, heat, and electricity (with Year 9)

- Earth and Space: gravity, satellites, the history of the stars, and the origin of the universe (with Year 10)

Each series consisted of between three and six lessons, and each lesson was for between 50 minutes and 1 hour and 40 minutes. In addition we collected data on a lesson on cells.

The video data was supplemented by four other types of data, each of which is briefly discussed below:

- Observation
- Texts used in the lessons (e.g. textbooks, worksheets)
- Texts produced by students and teachers in the lessons
- Focus groups with a sample of students (these were video recorded)

Video recording

Our theoretical perspective on communication, and more specifically on learning and teaching as a multimodal accomplishment, required methods of data collection which (i) facilitated a focus on a variety of modes in the classroom; (ii) could accurately record multimodal classroom interactions given their speed and complexity; and (iii) would provide a record from which all modes of communication could be transcribed.

The need for video recording to fulfil these requirements (Goodwin, 1981; Hanson, 1994) informed our decision to use it as the central data collection method in the project. We decided to use two video cameras as a consequence of our conception of teaching and learning as a dialogic process in which the teacher shapes meaning in response to an audience's (the students) response, and in which the students are seen as involved in learning as a process of remaking signs. One video camera was focused primarily on the activity of the teacher, the other on the activities of the students. When the students worked in small groups or pairs, one camera followed the teacher and captured the activity of the class as a whole, while the other focused on a small group or pairs of students. Over the series of lessons small groups or pairs were selected on the basis of pragmatic issues (e.g. the distance of their workbench from power plugs in the room, and lighting considerations) and to reflect the general social characteristics of the students in each class (in terms of gender and race). In total we recorded nineteen lessons (70 hours of video data).

The time-synchronized recording of teacher and students enabled the analysis to explore the dialogic nature of teacher-student interactivity. Video recording of the lessons captured the teachers' framing of learning experiences and the students' activity in relation to meaning-making, shaping of knowledge and literacy practices/skills.

Much has been written about video recording as a way of collecting data, in particular on the effect of the video camera on the data (see Lomax and Casey, 1998). Inevitably, the presence of the video camera initially produced much interest from the students. We explained to the students who would be likely to see the videos the purpose of the research, allowed them to look through the camera lens, and explained our reason for using video recording to collect the classroom data (in addition we offered them copies of the video tapes for their own viewing/reflection). One advantage of observing and recording a series of lessons over a number of weeks in each of the schools was that students and teachers appeared to become pretty well oblivious to the video camera. However, how one is to read this 'obliviousness' remains debatable.

Throughout the project we adopted a reflexive stance towards our use of the video data by attending to the manner in which the process of video recording in the classrooms constructed and produced the data collected. The video recordings were structured in that they began as the students entered the classroom and ended as they left it. The use of two cameras meant that we did not have to make decisions about who was the most pertinent communicator. However, even with two cameras the video recordings were selective; some elements of the classroom interactions were included and others were excluded. The data was structured by the ways in which the researchers set up and used the video cameras, for example through the positioning of the cameras in the classroom, the height and angle of the cameras, the movement or stillness of the camera. This reflexive approach enabled some of the theories and assumptions about classroom interaction, which underpinned our engagement in the field and the analysis of the data to be brought into play as 'analytical resources'.

In summary, we viewed the video data as a *representation* of the classroom, as a *video-text*. The presence of the two researchers and the video equipment made the video-text of the classroom inevitably different from that which the classroom would have been if we had not been there, but, we argue, not so contaminated by the research process as to make the video data invalid.

Observation

One class was selected and observed in each of the four schools. The research involved unstructured observation of the students and teachers across a series of lessons (alongside the video recording of the lesson). Observational notes were used to capture interactions which the video was unable to, for example the environment of the classroom as a whole (i.e. the spatial arrangement of objects, furniture and people in the classroom); exchanges between students off camera or spoken too quietly to be recorded; and some visual communication such as the teacher drawing on the whiteboard. Observation notes were taken to record key points where aspects of multimodal communication appeared to be particularly pertinent to the processes of teaching and learning, such as the shifts between modes, student and teacher engagement with different modes of communication, and conventional or ritualized communicative events. The researchers also took notes after the observation on potential routes of analysis and practical considerations for video recording the following lessons.

Texts used and produced in the lessons

A sample of texts produced or used by the teachers and students in each of the lessons we observed was collected. We analysed these texts in order to characterize and show evidence of how learning was shaped by the different demands for cognitive work made by each of the modes.

The texts (by which we mean the material forms combining visual, written, spoken and gestural modes in differing ways) were sampled so as to be representative of the range produced by students in each lesson. We collected these based on criteria including materiality, mode, layout, genre, style and agency. This sample included a variety of two- and three-dimensional texts such as textbooks, overhead projections, diagrams and worksheets used and produced by teachers; and students' drawings, concept maps, stories, models, test papers, investigations and evaluations. These texts were photographed and photocopied where possible.

Focus groups

Focus groups were conducted with the groups of students who were video recorded and who produced the texts in each of the schools. Seven focus groups were conducted with three to five students at the end of each series of lessons (and at the mid-point of a longer series of lessons).

The focus groups centred on the students' experiences and understanding of the key concepts in the lessons. This was investigated through general discussion, focusing on specific texts produced by students or through students conducting specific tasks designed as prompts. A series of prompts was designed based on the key themes of each series of lessons to access the students' understanding of abstract concepts taught in the lessons. A variety of prompts drew on the different signs and modes available in the lesson. Following a series of six lessons on energy we asked a group of students to make a poster on 'What is Energy?' In another school, in response to a lesson on cells in which they made models of a cell, we asked the students to use their models to explain what a cell is. On other occasions, video footage of the classroom was used as a prompt: in one school we asked the students to give a running commentary to accompany video footage of an experiment they had undertaken to explore their account of its purpose.

Multimodal transcription of video data

Transcription is a theory-laden practice. The level of detail of the transcript depends on the theoretical perspective of the transcriber (or the person instructing the transcriber). The transcription of speech into a written form involves the application of punctuation and other structures which display theories of language (e.g. the timing of pauses in transcripts for the purpose of conversation analysis) and the different questions researchers are addressing. While most transcripts of classroom data concentrate on the transcription of speech, our theoretical perspective of teaching and learning as multimodal processes demanded a transcription process which took account of how actional, visual and linguistic resources worked together to make meanings (a multimodal account). In order to achieve a multimodal transcript we produced a systematic account using descriptive dimensions highlighted as important both in our review of the literature and our engagement with the data. These included eye movement, gaze and direction of gaze, facial expression, hand and arm movement/configurations, the use of the whole body to make gestures, body posture, the position of people in the room and their use of space, the location and context of the action (e.g. the semiotics of architecture), the semiotic objects of action (Bateson, 1987; Bitti and Poggi, 1991; Merleau-Ponty, 1969; Crowder, 1996), and speech. Each of these aspects was recorded using time as an anchor.

The transcripts provided a thick, descriptive multimodal account of the video data. These transcriptions can be seen as a textual representation of our theoretical conceptualization of the relations between modes; they are the product of an interpretative process between us and the video data. The process of transcribing the video data involved viewing the tapes many times: with image only, with sound only, and with both sound and image. Through intensive group viewing of the data using the concept of frame, we built a description of classroom interactions (the transcription process focused on all modes). This information was either represented entirely in written and visual form (Figure 1.1) or in written form (Figure 1.2). The decision of what form to represent information in depended on the intensity of the information and the focus of the analysis.

	POSITION	BODY
face, curved and closed together and you keep an amount of air (teacher cups her hands together) in a small space.		'turns carefully'
'Say in my hand I've got a certain amount of gas in my hand, OK, if I open my hand, then the particles that make up the gas, (Teacher separates her hands suddenly, and then pauses) they go all over the place, they fill up the room, they move all around the room, OK?'		' walks slowly, carefully, 'holding' hands in front movement all located in hands / arms. Body 'tense - firm'
T: If I do that to a solid (teacher cups a piece of chalk in her hand, pauses, then moves one hand away) has it moved anywhere? S: No. T: No, OK.		swivells around, picks up chalk
If I've got a liquid, (teacher gets a plastic container and a plastic 'squirter' of water) If I squeeze the container, okay. (teacher squeezes water into the container. It sounds like passing water.)	top	
(Laughter) T: Okay (Laughter)		
T: You can sqeeze the water, it flows, but does it go all over, the place? (teacher 'rolls' the container in front of the students) S: It drops.		

FIGURE 1.1 *Transcript in written and visual form.*

FACE / GAZE	OBJECT	HAND AND ARM LANGUAGE
Left and right	'air'	① "Keep an amount of air" ② hold for a few secs. in a small space — gestures generated by instance not wholly by convention / hands as walls
Directly at class		③ ④ ⑤ 'move all around' / left hand keeps still / 'fill up the room'
	Chalk requires pupils to imagine chalk particle 'dust?'	⑥ takes hand away / arm drops to side
Looks at jug and water; holds away from herself	Jug and distilled water bottle, water.	⑦
		Drops arm down by side of body
		Raise to position in ⑦

FIGURE 1.1 *(Continued).*

Time	Action	Verbal
11.31	B: lights fuel with Bunsen	
	A: picks up clock and sets it	
	A: holds hands together as if holding fuel with tongs	A: Am I supposed to keep on holding it like that?
		B: No, I don't think so.
	A: leaves bench	A: I'm going to go and ask miss.
	D: picks up worksheet and reads	T: No. Once it's lit then that's all right.
		B: See!
	A: returns, lowers bottom clamp	A: Make it a bit more lower.
	E: points with his glasses at the experiment	E: Check the temperature.
		D: It's about 30.
	A: points at B	A: Keep an eye on the temperature.
	All look at equipment	
	B: looks at thermometer	B: It's going up,
	raises his fist	31 yeah, 36, 39, 41,
11.32	starts to dance	50, 51, 52
	A: checks clock	A: Going to hold it for three minutes.
	B: puts his glasses on, leans in	B: 61, 2, 3, 4, 5
	A: gets his exercise book	A: I'll write the results down, yeah?
		B: Okay.
	A: points at table	A: Am I supposed to tick it? Name of sample tested.
	A: looks at B	What's the sample?
		B: Thingy, energy cube.
	A: leaves table	A: Miss?
		A: Tablet solid.
		E: Fuel solid.
	D: brings back box and gives it to A	A: Metafuel they call it.
		B: No, solid fuel tablet.
		A: Metafuel.
	T: arrives, holds box, reads	T: Metafuel.
11.33	A: writes, reads table	A: Easy to ignite?
	looks at experiment, writes	B: Yes.
	reads table in exercise book	A: Does it keep burning?
	bends down and looks	Yeah.
	at experiment	Is there smoke?
	looks at B	B: Can you see any smoke?
	writes	B: No, there's only a flame.
	looks at equipment	

FIGURE 1.2 *Transcript in written form.*

Time	Action	Verbal
	B: puts splint in flame picks up clock	A: B, leave it, B, leave it. A: Oh, we leave it for 4 minutes, Oh, it's quite burning now. It's nearly 3 minutes. We're supposed to leave it burning now till it stops.
11.34	B: walks around, looks, takes glasses off, looks at thermometer	
	All lean forward and look	B: What is it? What is it?
	D: looks at thermometer	D: It's over one hundred. E: Leave it. A: Leave it until it stops burning.
	All leaning forward, looking	B: See how long it takes, init?

FIGURE 1.2 *(Continued)*

Data analysis

The sample of texts was analysed using a social semiotic approach. These texts were approached as concrete traces of the cognitive work involved in their production: that is, treated as semiotically expressed responses. As described earlier in the section *Rethinking Learning,* these texts were analysed as one type of evidence in order to understand the teaching and learning processes engaged with in the science classroom. That is, they were analysed in terms of the decisions students engaged with in their production (this information was elicited through observation of the production of the text and focus groups). Qualitative analysis of these texts focused on the students' production of them in relation to the following dimensions:

1   The students' selection of elements from the lesson, that is their inclusion and exclusion of elements (semiotic resources) made available by the teacher or as the resources in the classroom.

2   The students' adaptation of elements introduced by the teacher or the resources in the classroom.

3 The students' introduction of elements not made available by the teacher or the resources in the classroom (i.e. from outside of the domain of the classroom).

4 The students' arrangement of these elements into texts, their 'design' (see New London Group, 1996; Cope and Kalantzis, 2000).

5 The representational modes used by the students.

6 The physical characteristics of the texts – their materiality.

These dimensions were examined particularly in relation to the question of learning and to the cognitive consequences, potentials and constraints which texts of this kind would have, with a subsidiary focus on the variations and similarities between student texts.

Successive viewing of the video data played a large role in the generation of understandings, and the first viewings guided the preliminary analysis of the data. The process of logging and organizing the video data yielded insights simply through our intensive engagement with the material. It generated new meanings, and drew attention to important aspects of communication.

The video recordings of the classroom interactions were classified into discrete analytical units by viewing the video data alongside written transcripts, observation notes, preliminary ideas and by applying categories of rhetorical frame once these had been developed. Gross shifts in posture, position, communicative mode and content were read as the start and end markers of these analytical units (Scheflen, 1973; Bateson, 1987) which were crucial in the definition and establishing of rhetorical frames. More specifically, these rhetorical frames were formally marked by a configuration of a range of factors including the starting point for the lesson; the way the teacher positions him- or herself and the students in relation to knowledge (e.g. in relation to students' existing experiences); the choice of content; the dominant communicative mode; the means, props, or objects used in the lesson; teacher and student agency and activities; teacher and students' posture and movement in the classroom; the type of interchange (e.g. monologue or question and answer sequences); and lexical style.

In this way the tapes were catalogued into chunks of data (a minimum of one minute up to a maximum of 15 minutes in length) which provided us with a descriptive account of the rhetorical framing and reframing of each of the videotaped lessons.

These analytically and descriptively established units (rhetorical frames) were then classified further according to the theoretical concept of mode to produce a 'modal catalogue' of headings under which they might be further analysed: multimodality, visual communicative mode, the objects of action, forms of knowledge, and students' sign-making. Due to the intensive nature of multimodal analysis we selected a representative range of case-study examples according to the science education topics which they focused on, their rhetorical framing, their foregrounded mode, object of action, and shaping of knowledge. The case-studies served to show how each mode contributed to the realization of a range of rhetorical intentions across a range of topics in the science classroom, and how these modes contribute differently to the shaping of students' knowledge.

These examples of multimodal interactions were analysed as detailed 'trails' in order to capture the learning and teaching practices in which students and teachers engage. The analysis sought to identify the communicational and representational potentials made available to teachers and students in the science classroom. The concepts outlined earlier in this chapter provided us with a range of research tools with which to begin to prise open the multimodal environment of the science classroom. These included medium, mode, materiality, functional specialism, (Halliday's notion of) grammar, meaning-making functions, interest, rhetorical framing, the rhetorical orchestration of meaning, and learning as a dynamic process of sign-making.

The first stage of our analysis involved exploring our data by attending to each of the modes of communication operating in the classroom separately using these conceptual tools. This was to provide a detailed characterization of the uses of each of the modes including what in a mode lent itself to semiotic exploitation (the materiality of the medium as much as its cultural/historical shaping); how the mode was organized or structured and what categories of elements functioned in relation to these structures; the patterns of meaning-making in the interaction; and the characteristics of the dialogue of interaction between students and teacher. This involved intensive viewing, the transcription of all modes, and classification of the data into meaning functions in order to explore how modes realized different semiotic meanings.

Thus we classified the ways in which action represented what was going on in the science classroom (Halliday's ideational meaning); how action could be used to bring about interactions and relations between teachers and students (interpersonal meaning); and how action was used to form meaningful communicationally effective texts (textual meaning). Textual meanings were realized in many ways through actions, for instance, through a holding gesture in a lesson on particles which textually anchored the action in the spoken discourse. The teacher's body movement gave textual meaning by marking space and providing a sense of 'marked happenings', while simultaneously textual transitions in several modes mapped out changing parameters and meanings. Through this process we generated semantically motivated classifications of action.

In the second stage of our analysis, detailed exploration of modes in interaction was in focus; here we examined how each of the modes interacted in the classroom to make meaning. This process entailed further viewing and comparisons across the meaning functions of each mode by examining how with co-occurring modes one can read the meaning of one mode in relation to the others. In order to do this we focused on aspects of meaning in four main ways:

1   The role of different kinds of semiotic objects in the classroom – what types of things were manipulated, pointed at, and how did teachers' and students' interaction with these objects bring them into existence, or momentarily transform them?

2   The modes in relation to each other – through examining the co-occurring modes and viewing modes across the lesson we identified repetitions, reiterations, and transformations of modes. Through this comparison of incidence we were able to identify what Scheflen (1974) calls customary acts, i.e. acts that happen in a particular context at a particular time and have an established function.

3   The representational and communicational tension between modes – e.g. What was said verbally and performed through action? Why might action have been introduced at a particular point in a lesson? What did it enable the teacher or student to do? Through this process of comparison and contrast we attempted to unpick the role of each mode in the communicative event seen holistically.

4   The contexts of use of the mode of gesture in order to identify the functional meanings of a gesture in relation to larger units of communication – e.g. Did the gesture open up the dialogue, or manage the transition from one rhetorical frame to another? Viewing of the synchronized video tapes of teacher and student activity enabled us to explore this question very usefully, because we could see the dialogic and collaborative nature of multimodal communication between teacher and students in the science classroom.

The focus groups conducted with students were analysed using (lightly handled) social semiotic and discourse analytic approaches. The emphasis was on the dynamic ways in which the relationship between learning and mode was worked in the classroom environment. In this way the focus groups provided another source of data with which to track the students' meaning-making/learning processes in the science classroom. They were used primarily as a source of information to inform our analyses of the video recordings of the classrooms and of the texts produced by students.

2

Multimodality

Introduction

In the previous chapter we noted that language is widely taken to be the dominant mode of communication in learning and teaching. Image, gesture and action are generally considered illustrative supports to the 'real thing'. Our observation of teaching and learning in the science classroom casts doubt on this assumption. In the teaching and learning of science it is common practice for teachers to use demonstration, experiment and images to explain phenomena, and to set tasks which require a visual or actional response, for example the production of concept maps, diagrams and three-dimensional models, and experiment or investigation. We suggest that the linguistic focus of much previous educational research on talk, reading, and writing in the classroom has been both an effect of this common sense and has served to confirm the dominant view of learning as a primarily linguistic accomplishment.

The increasing prevalence of multimodal texts (texts-as-objects which use more than one mode of meaning-making) and multimodal communication raises a crucial question: is an analytical procedure which attends to communication as a purely linguistic event capable of providing plausible accounts of the communicational functions of such texts?

Once this question is raised, several others immediately crop up: do other semiotic modes show regularities such as those in language? Do other modes relate to cultural and social organization? Are these modes used to express social factors like power and ideology? How do modes interact with one another to make meaning? What effects, if any, do these modes have on the very forms of language itself and hence on the theorization of what language is and can be? The focus of this chapter is on a multimodal approach to classroom interaction and the full repertoire of meaning-making resources which students and teachers bring to the classroom (actional, visual, and linguistic resources), and on how these are organized to make meaning.

We demonstrate the application of multimodal analysis to an example of teaching and learning in the science classroom with a focus on how each mode makes a partial meaning in isolation and interweaves with the others to make the full meaning of the event or text.

A multimodal approach to communication

Here we briefly restate some points of principle made in the previous chapter, just to frame the discussion that follows. Three theoretical points inform our account of multimodal communication in the classroom. First, mediums are shaped and organized into a range of meaning-making systems in order to articulate the meanings demanded by the social requirements of different communities; these we call *modes*. All modes make meanings differently, and the meanings made are not always available to or understood by all readers. Second, the meaning of language-as-speech or language-as-writing, as of all other modes, is always interwoven with the meanings made by all the other modes simultaneously present and operating in the communicative context, and this interaction itself produces meaning. Third, what can be considered a communicative mode is more or less always open – systems of meaning are fluid, modes of communication develop and change in response to the communicative needs of society, new modes are created, existing modes are transformed.

Moreover the question of whether X is a mode or not is a question specific to a particular community. As laypersons we may regard visual image to be a mode, while a professional photographer will say that photography has rules and practices, elements and materiality quite distinct from that of painting, and that the two are distinct modes. It is unproductive to enter into general debates on this outside of the quite specific contexts of social groups and their semiotic practices. The point is important here because, as we suggested in the previous chapter, the community of science (educators) may well have developed modes which are not recognized as such outside that community. Learning science is then in one part learning to recognize the modes of that community.

Halliday's (1985) social theory of communication provided the starting point for our exploration of multimodal teaching and learning in the science classroom. He argues that in verbal interactions with others we have at our disposal networks of options (or sets of semiotic alternatives) which are realized through sets of options of the semantic system. The elements of the semantic system of language are differentiated so as to reflect the social function of the utterance as representation, interaction and message, and are realized in language by the lexico-grammar. The principle underpinning this model is that language is as it is because of the functions (meanings) it has evolved to realize. It is organized to function with respect to social interests and demands placed on it by those who use it in their social lives. In this way language can be understood as the cultural shaping of a medium (sound in the case of language-as-speech) into regular forms for representation (grammar) in which it becomes the material resource (as signifiers) for meanings in the constant new making of signs.

A multimodal and social semiotic approach starts from the position that visual communication, gesture, and action have evolved through their social usage into articulated or partially articulated semiotic systems in the same way that language has. Extending Halliday's theory we suggest that each of these modes has been developed as a network of interlocking resources for making signs. The alternatives selected within these networks of meaning can then be seen as *traces* of a sign-maker's decision-making about what is the most apt and plausible signifier for the expression of the intended meaning in a given context. It is one expression of the sign-maker's *interest* (Halliday, 1985; Kress, 1997).

From this perspective, we understand teaching and learning in the science classroom to be the material expression of the motivated (cognitive and affective) choices of teachers and students from among the meaning-making resources available in a particular situation (the science classroom in this study) at a given moment.

The multimodal environment of the science classroom

This section provides a case-study account of the ways in which writing, gesture, image and speech were used by a teacher to construct the entity 'blood' and to reposition the students' 'take on the world'. This account focuses on a detailed description of the first of five lessons on the circulation of the blood with Year 8 students in a London Community and Technical College. First we offer a description of the lesson which draws attention to its multimodal characteristics.

The lesson consisted of two half-hour parts (separated by a lunch break). The conception of the movement of blood as a cycle was established by the teacher in the first part of the lesson. He used different representations of types of cycles to do this, including the repetition of cyclical gestures, the conceptual cycle of the process of the blood (e.g. the recurring 'cleaning' of the blood), visual cycles in images, verbs of going and coming to discuss the movement of the blood, and the visual cycle created by the interaction of the cut-out section of a model of the human body and the teacher's gestures on it. The teacher's speech and the images he used, together with his gestures and his other actions, combined to establish the 'key players' in the process, and the heart as a central player. The teacher's communicative shifts between modes in the first half of the lesson are summarized in Table 2.1.

As Table 2.1 shows, the teacher used a range of modes to construct the entity of 'blood circulation'. Initially his speech was foregrounded; he then used gesture to locate the processes he described and to introduce direction and movement. The teacher

Table 2.1 The teacher's communicative shifts between modes in the first half of the lesson

	Summary of meaning made in mode		
Time	Speech/writing	Action	Visual
12.20	Register – control	Stillness – control	Model of human body on desk – locates lesson visually in 'human'
12.21	Instruction – sets agenda	Distributes books – sets agenda	Image and text in book – sets agenda (specifically)
12.22	Revision – outlines key players	Gesture – shows location, directionality	
12.23	Names parts and functions	Manipulates model – introduces parts	Visual classification of parts and processes
12.25	Narrative – blood circulation	Locate narrative in model	Relates parts to whole
12.26	Instructions	Gesture links diagram to model, and model to teacher's body – layered effect	Diagram in book Cycle constructed Key players Knowledge to be gained
12.28	Instructions – sets agenda	Points at questions to be answered	Diagram
12.30	Writes on the whiteboard – frames lesson		Diagram
12.31	Students write answers in textbook – construct process as written narrative		Diagram – directionality, location, process, route

(Continued)

Table 2.1 (Continued)

	Summary of meaning made in mode		
Time	Speech/writing	Action	Visual
12.36	Further instructions	Points to another diagram	Diagram – directionality, abstracted, transformation (colour), symmetry
12.37	Narrates the cycle	Shows direction of movement	Diagram in book
12.38	Students work individually		
12.41	Summary of cycle	Manipulates model	Model – location, direction, route

then shifted the attention from his speech (and body) to a model of the human body. His manipulation of the model enabled him to place the organs named in his verbal narrative in relation to one another, locate the process in the human body and to visually classify these parts and processes. He then shifted attention from the model to a diagram in a textbook. Through gesture he linked the diagram to the model, and the model to his body. His verbal narrative and gesture linked the three visual resources – body, model and diagram – as a series of representations of the body. Each representational mode enabled the unfolding of a different view of the body. In the process each mode provided a deeper view 'inside the human' and removed another layer of the individuality of what was being represented, changing the representation of the human body to a more general abstracted one.

The diagram abstracted the representation further by removing the context of the process represented visually. In this way the process of the teacher's shift from action on the body to the model and diagram created a layered effect, a visual continuum of depth. The abstraction of the blood cycle represented in the textbook image articulated the final product of this process of abstraction, from the teacher's body as 'individual' and whole to the dislocated abstraction represented diagrammatically. In short, the meaning central to this as 'science' was made by the way in which the modes were orchestrated by the teacher as rhetor.

In the second half of the lesson, the conception of the circulation of the blood as a circle became a part of the 'local epistemology' – what at that point the teacher assumed to be known and could be taken to count as a 'ground of knowledge' (Ogborn *et al.,* 1998). The second part of the lesson started with an image drawn on the whiteboard (Figure 2.1). The teacher offered a verbal narrative of the circulation of the blood, which he transposed through gesture onto this image. This is given in the box below Figure 2.1.

The teacher then offered a more complex verbal description of the cycle of the blood as a double loop with blood going to the lungs and the rest of the body. He added this second loop to his initial drawing on the whiteboard (Figure 2.2).

Having described the route of the blood the teacher placed a model of the human body on the bench in front of him (Figure 2.3).

He handled the model heart while describing the blood's movement through the heart and the contraction of the heart muscles. Cyclicity was represented by the teacher's animation of the model and by his use of verbs of going and coming.

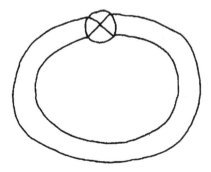

FIGURE 2.1 *Image on the whiteboard.*

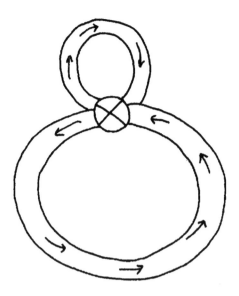

FIGURE 2.2 *Adapted image on the whiteboard.*

Speech	Action
We can think about it as a circle	points at heart, traces finger around circle
of blood like this, going round,	returns hand to heart, draws on arrows
and at various points, say, the	places opened hand at left of diagram
lungs are here, the small intestine	places opened hand at bottom left of diagram
here, and the cells are here, the	places opened hand bottom right of diagram
kidneys up here, okay so it's going	places opened hand at top right of diagram
all the way around and what	draws arrows on circle, points at heart
it needs is something to start	bends elbows, arms at side, 'bellows' action
pumping it again to give it a bit	makes 'bellows' action three times
more motion to go around okay.	puts pen lid on

The teacher then directed the students to look at an image in their textbook (Figure 2.4). He used his finger to trace the process of the circulation of the blood on the image, providing a multimodal (visual, verbal and gestural) summary of the lesson.

FIGURE 2.3 *Teacher manipulating model of human body.*

Speech	Action
Now if we look at that on our	places model on front desk
model you can actually see here	stands behind model, arms in front
the heart has four main blood	picks up heart, points at heart
vessels okay now . . .	puts heart back in model
and if we take the front off, you	takes front panel off heart
can see what's going on inside,	lifts heart out of model to in front of him
basically blood is coming round	sticks out index finger, traces loop from
from the rest of the body into	his head to heart, puts finger in chamber
this first chamber here . . . okay	moves finger about in chamber
it goes from this chamber into	moves finger to next chamber
this bottom chamber on this	
side. That's where the first pump	slowly contracts hand into a fist, twice
happens.	

Speech	Action
Now you can see that on your diagram in your books exactly the same process here this is the blood coming back from the rest of the body it comes into the first chamber, down into the big chamber at the bottom, gets squeezed up into the lungs, back down again into the, this chamber here, down into the big one at the bottom again, squeezed out and around. You can trace it with your finger down – up – in – and out.	picks up textbook, moves away from model holds book at neck level, with finger traces arrows on diagram from bottom to top traces route into chamber traces route into next chamber makes a fist action traces route up to lungs traces route down into chamber traces route down into chamber makes a fist action traces whole route quickly with finger

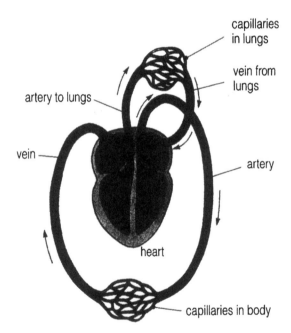

FIGURE 2.4 *Image from the textbook used in the lesson (Keith Johnson, Sue Adamson and Gareth Williams,* Spotlight Science 8, *Stanley Thornes Ltd, 1994).*

Next, the teacher instructed the students to complete a series of activities from their textbook which focused on the function of the different organs, in particular of the heart, in the process of blood circulation.

Table 2.2 summarizes the teacher's use and meaning of modes in the second half of the lesson. Over the course of the lesson the process-entity 'blood circulation' emerged from the interweaving

Table 2.2 The teacher's communicative shifts between modes in the second half of the lesson

Time	Speech/writing	Action	Visual
13.15		Draws image on board	Image on board
13.16	Narrative, Q and A about cycle, heart	Gestures locate organs from his body onto image on the board, draws arrows	Image on board – directionality
13.17	Narrative – not so simple	Acts out pump action	Relates action to image
13.18	New narrative of cycle	Acts out narrative on body Gestures locate parts to image, movement	Amends image – new visual directionality locates narrative
13.19	Repeats new narrative, new parts named (heart chambers)	Manipulates model Relates model to body via movement	Model – direction, location, entity
13.21	Repeats new narrative	Gestures trace direction. Acts out 'pump'	Diagram – abstract representation of cycle

(Continued)

Table 2.2 (Continued)

Time	Speech/writing	Action	Visual
13.22	Q and A – explanations	Gesture – emphasis	
13.29	Instructions	Holds book, indicates questions	Book
13.30	Students work (write)		
13.35	Summarizes lesson		
13.37	Instructions Homework	Gestures emphasize key points	

of meanings created by the teacher's shifting between the modes. In the second half of the lesson the foregrounded image of a single cycle on the whiteboard (Figure 2.1) provided the visual evidence both of simplicity and of abstraction. Visually this opened up the explanatory need for the teacher's more complex verbal narrative. This contrast is a reflection of the history of the discovery of blood, which was once thought of as a single loop and later understood to be a double loop. The verbal narrative laid across the image, and the teacher's gestures temporarily placed the named organs on the image of the route of circulation. The teacher's verbal and gestural correction was then replaced by the permanence of an amended drawing (Figure 2.2). The teacher then repeated the narrative of the complex cycle of the blood, first in relation to the model and then in relation to the diagram. The teacher set the students to work individually on the questions in the textbook and instructed them on their homework. Finally, the teacher summarized the lesson in a verbal monologue. The function of each of the modes in the second half of the lesson is discussed in detail below.

Mode and meaning

Speech: Creating difference

At the beginning of the second half of the lesson the teacher contrasted the initial schematic verbal description of the blood's circuit (developed in the first half of the lesson) with a second more detailed version of 'what actually happens'. He says, 'It would be very simple if that is what it was like. . . . But it's not quite that simple. . .'.

The contrast was achieved by a juxtaposition of the teacher's more detailed verbal description with the image of the abstract cycle drawn on the whiteboard. The contrast between what the teacher said, the abstract diagram of one circuit, and what he went on to say 'actually happens', set up the need for an explanation.

The image on the whiteboard: A visual backdrop

The image provided the starting point for the lesson and formed the ground on which the other modes were developed. The image on the whiteboard (Figure 2.1) presented a view of the circulatory system as a highly abstracted entity. The image could be adapted and provided an abstract visual map on which to read the verbal explanations the teacher offered. As the teacher went on to mention the places on the route of the blood (lungs, small intestine, cells, kidneys) he did not draw them on the image, rather his speech and gesture served to project a 'transparent (imagined) overlay' of detail onto the abstract image.

The materiality of the whiteboard and the mode of gesture together afforded a flexibility which enabled the organs to be presented in a transient way which evaporated once it had served its purpose. In this way the teacher's engagement with the materiality of the whiteboard avoided him having to change the position of the lungs when he later extended the image to reflect a more complex view of the circuit of the blood. Similarly it obviated both the problem of representing the 'organ' and the placing of it in one location on the diagram. In this mode these were questions which could not arise.

The adapted image (Figure 2.2) provided a visual analogy of a figure of eight which translated the teacher's verbal explanation into an abstracted image rooted in the everyday, which served as a memory tool.

The two-dimensionality of the visual medium reorganized the representation of the heart and lungs ('in front' became 'up', 'behind' became 'down'). The framework developed by Kress and van Leeuwen (1996) to look at composition as meaningful (that is, the compositional values in a two-dimensional rectangular space of: ideal – top; real – bottom; left – given; and right – new) was applied to the image. This analysis suggested the composition of the image provided information about the process and direction of the blood's circulation around the body. The left section of the image was used for the blood needing oxygen going to the heart where it will get it – so the area of the 'given' was used to represent 'before'. (That is, the 'given' of the situation, the issue which causes the question to be put in the first place, is that the body needs oxygen, the heart is the carrier of the oxygen, and the problem which starts the issue is: there is no oxygen.) The right-hand section of the image, the 'new', was used to represent 'after': the blood has oxygen. So the left had the meaning of 'old', 'used up', 'waiting', and 'coming'. The top and bottom of the images corresponded with the opposition: 'source' vs 'sink' – the 'supply' vs 'things supplied'. The heart and lungs at the top were 'source'. The organs, etc. at the bottom of the images were 'use'. So the space of the 'ideal' was used to represent 'source' (in Hallidayan terms, 'ideal' was used to realize 'source'; in semiotic terms 'ideal' was used as the signifier for the signified 'source'); 'actual' was used to realize 'use'.

Manipulating the model: Locating the discussion in a physical setting

The two-dimensional images used by the teacher represented the schematic knowledge of how to think. The model (as shown in Figure 2.3) presented a sense of the scientific process of exploration; going deeper into the subject. 'Inside' is brought 'out' onto the surface (literally). The model is used to take that surface view inside, to show where exactly a schematic process works. What is being explored is how the actual contains the ideal.

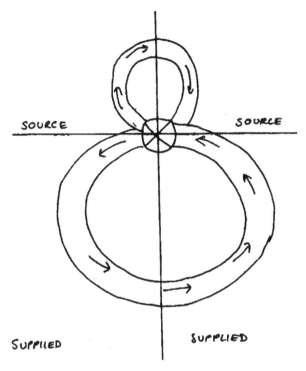

FIGURE 2.5 *Compositional information value of the teacher's diagram.*

The model made visible the usually unseen insides of the human body and in the process transformed the everyday human body into the scientific entity 'human body'. Gender was made invisible through the equalizing of difference (e.g. the model had both female and male sexual organs and an androgynous face). Colour was used as a visual representation of the transformative process of blood circulation: grey/blue for 'used blood' and red for 'oxygenated blood'.

The model presented the spatial relation between the parts (the organs) and the whole (the human body) in a more complex dimensional relationship than the two-dimensional representation afforded. The model represented depth and layered relationships between the organs in the teacher's narrative. The static, solid materiality of the model limited its role in the explanation of a dynamic and organic process by representing the organs as hard, lifeless things that do not move. However, the limitation in this mode also enabled the heart to be physically handled in ways that actual hearts could not be.

Action: Made dynamic

The teacher's gestures highlighted the dynamic nature of the circulation of the blood and the pumping of the heart, and this compensated for the limitations of the image and the model. He used pantomimic gestures throughout the lesson to enact the movement of the different imagined entities the students were required to imagine: the body, heart, valves and blood. At the start of the segment he used his body as a model to provide a physical location for the circulation of the blood; he later held his hand flat open in a pantomimic act of being winded and shocked, demonstrating in gesture the physical effect of the content of his speech, 'It's got no oxygen in it okay, where does it need to go to get oxygen?'

He used his arms and hands to demonstrate the movement of the heart and valves and later, when he used the model to demonstrate the flow of the blood through the heart, he gave a physical representation of blood by making a lasso-like motion with his index finger. This introduced a sense of dynamic to the static visual representations in the diagram, the model and the image in the textbook.

The teacher's use of his body realized an interpersonal function: he used his body as a visual location for the verbal and visual information which he provided in the lesson. In connecting the real and the schematic he oriented the students in a way which was suggestive of the need for them to think about their bodies not as they usually experience them, but to imagine their bodies' internal structure. Later in the segment, the teacher's use of his body provided a living location for the model. He stood behind the model, his arm on its shoulder, embracing the model in a way which presented the model as an aspect of himself. In this way his body provided an outside for the insides, a real for the analysed. The teacher's use of his body and gesture dynamized the human body, while the model served to classify it. The teacher used his body to show how the human body looks to us. The model represented the body as analysed into parts. The image represented the body parts analytically in terms of their function. Thus there were three levels of analysis of the body within the lesson: movement, parts and functions.

The teacher repeatedly made two gestures throughout the lesson: a circular motion with his hand and arm, and a contracting gesture made with his hand and arms pressed against his body. He made the circular gesture in relation to his body, by making a circular movement around his upper torso; he used his arm and hand to trace the circles of the image on the whiteboard, and he used his arms to encircle the model and to show the circular route of the imagined blood from the heart. Finally he traced the circular route of the blood on the image in the textbook. At one point, he made this circular gesture a total of 16 times in five minutes. The gesture emphasized the movement of the blood as a cycle. During the same five-minute segment he made the contracting gesture, holding his palm wide open and closing it in a grabbing motion to form a fist, a total of 23 times. This contraction gesture represented the pump action of the heart. In this way the teacher realized two elements of meaning in the ideational function – 'cyclical movement' and 'contraction', two key themes of the lesson. The teacher's repetition of the circular and contracting gesture provided a rhythmic backdrop for the lesson which enabled movement across different modes and media to achieve coherence.

The image in the textbook:
A stable summary

The image in the textbook (Figure 2.4) serves the function of providing a stable summary (a summary of the knowledge at issue in canonical form) of the two-dimensional and three-dimensional images and actions presented by the teacher. It offers a topographical representation of the heart and the circulation of the blood which draws on the visual analogy of a figure of eight and presents it in a form that allowed the knowledge introduced by the teacher's enactment of the model to make full sense.

Orchestration of meaning

The modes interacted in different ways throughout the lesson and different modes were foregrounded at particular points. At times the teacher's speech was independently coherent, at others the meaning of his speech was entirely intertwined with his action, to the extent that neither his speech nor his actions were coherent when viewed independently of one another. In short, each mode contributed to the meaning being made.

Throughout the first half of the lesson the model was made salient through the teacher's manipulation of it to display the parts named in his narrative. The model was then backgrounded by the teacher as he focused on the textbook diagram, and later he went on to use his body as a canvas for explanation. The model was later foregrounded again, functioning as the location of the teacher's narrative in order to indicate the direction and route of the blood's cycle. These shifts can be seen as one effect of the material potentials and limitations of the model to convey the required meaning. As the focus of the teacher's communication shifted from one of 'organic movement' to the need to explain blood circulation as a process which unfolds over time, the teacher shifted from the mode of action to the mode of speech. Within the lesson each of the modes came to realize specific meanings (in line with their functional specialization in the science classroom) both through the teacher's development of practice and in the lesson itself.

The teacher's speech was the foregrounded mode in the first part of the lesson and was coherent without reference to the images which he introduced and his gestures. He verbally and visually set up the issue for discussion in the first part of the lesson by building the notion of the blood flow as a cycle. In the second part of the lesson he presented and then refuted his initial explanation of how the heart works, creating the need for an explanation which he then provided. The teacher's use of image and action alongside his speech realized the continuous cyclical movement of the blood and the contraction of the heart. His speech combined with his actions and use of image to build a schematized version of the circulation. The figure-of-eight image offered a basic map with which to read what was to follow in the lesson.

Standing in front of the image on the whiteboard he introduced the model of the inside of the human body using his body as a model for the outside. In this way his body mediated the transition between the image on the board and the model on the bench in a layering way – his body overlaid the image; the model overlaid his body. His speech, gesture and the concrete model were fully integrated. His speech provided an explanation through narrative, his gesture indicated the players and acted out and dynamized the verbal narrative, and the model provided an analytical representation of the body as the physical location for the discussion and the relationship between the parts and the whole. Finally, the textbook image offered a more detailed visual summary of all that had happened.

The different semiotic modes within the lesson worked together to form a coherent text through a range of textual features. The teacher used modes to produce similarity and contrast, including the schematic vs actual, inside vs outside and idea vs object contrasts. Repetition of the verbal, visual and gestural description of the blood cycle was another way in which the modes worked together to create coherence. In the second half of the lesson the verbal description was repeated seven times, the visual depiction three times and the actional cycles 16 times. Coherence was achieved by the telling of a narrative that went across and drew on different semiotic modes, each mode contributing to the whole communicative event. For example, at one point in the narrative of the blood circulation (13.19 in Table 2.2) the actor (blood) was carried in the teacher's speech, the physical location of the action was provided in the model, and the teacher's manipulation of the model was the representation of the process (movement of the blood). At other times, it was the teacher's synchronization of different semiotic modes which produced meaning. For example, at one point in the lesson (13.21) the synchronization of the teacher's speech, his action of tracing the arrows on the textbook image of the blood's movement around the heart, and the textbook image itself worked in combination to produce an abstract directional map of the process entity 'blood circulation'.

Multimodal repositioning

The teacher's use of different modes repositioned the students in relation to the human body. Here we focus on the second half of the lesson. The teacher's talk and his use of the image on the whiteboard required the students to imagine themselves inside the body. The teacher's gesture and his use of his body as a model asked them to imagine themselves as observers outside of the body. By acting out the pumping action of the heart, the teacher, through his gesture, took the students a layer deeper, so that they were in the heart seeing the movement of the valves. Shifting attention to the model, the teacher pointed out and handled the organs, a modern-day dissection reminiscent of an autopsy. This required the students to imagine the model as once moving, as if they were medical students looking at a dead body – observers of the transformation from the process of experiencing the body as an external entity to experiencing it as an internal entity. The textbook image required the students to imagine the context 'the rest of the body'. Finally, the homework which the teacher set, to write 'as a blood cell' of their journey around the body, required the students to imagine being a blood cell. In this way each of the modes worked together to achieve the rhetorical repositioning of students and the construction of the entity 'the human body'. In summary, throughout the second half of the lesson the students were required to shift their view of the body between an internal entity and an external one.

Internal: Talk and image – body as process
External: Gesture – body as location
Internal – deeper: Pantomimic gestures – body as movement, heart as pump
External – distant: Manipulation of the model – body as parts
Internal – deeper still: Homework – blood as entity (cell)

Each shift involved the students metaphorically re-entering the body at a deeper level and exiting at a more distant level. This movement echoed the process of science as immersion and observation.

The students were required to do different types of imaginative work in order to make sense of the different aspects of the circulatory system presented by the teacher. The image required the students to imagine the inside of the body as a circuit and the movement of blood around this circuit; to envisage the size and position of organs, and the relationships between them in a highly abstract fashion; to think of the internal organs in a circuit, and of the cells as collected up into one place (like an organ); to transform the relationship between the heart and lungs from a three-dimensional relationship where the lungs are in front of the heart into a two-dimensional relationship where the lungs are above the heart (i.e. to translate spatial relationships so that front became up, behind became down). The teacher's use of gesture and of his body as a model required the students to imagine what goes on 'beneath the skin' and to envisage the organs and their movement. The model required the students to think about different elements of the cycle besides those which required speech and image (for example, the relationship between the organs is realized in the model, the setting for the action). The teacher's actions with the model provided the movement and direction of actions in the narrative and required the students to envisage the agent of this action – the blood. In short, each mode both repositioned the students in relation to 'the human body', and demanded different cognitive work of them. Through this interweaving of modes the complex meaning of this part of the science curriculum was realized.

Conclusion

Taking a multimodal approach highlights the complexity of science classroom interaction and the tasks of pedagogy. Here our aim is to describe the range of meaning-making resources available in the science classroom which contribute to these processes in order to better understand them. When teachers speak they nearly always simultaneously deploy other semiotic resources for meaning-making. Teachers often use gesture alongside their speech to draw attention to images and other elements within the classroom as references. Likewise, writing deploys visual, graphological and typographical semiotics. We have shown that in the multimodal environment of the science classroom the meaning of what is spoken or written does not reside purely in language, but in the complex interweaving between the linguistic, visual and actional resources which teachers and students draw on in their communication.

We hope the detailed analysis above demonstrates that the work of the teacher and of the students in their task of re-envisaging the world is not accomplished purely through language. The lesson drew on a variety of modes which were themselves organized in a shifting hierarchy. Speech was never the only mode; at times it was accompanied by visual communication, at others by gesture, sometimes by both. Sometimes the teacher's speech was foregrounded, at other times it shifted between foreground and background. In this multimodal text, the modes interacted and interplayed to produce a coherent text through repetition, synchronization, similarity and contrast.

We suggest that, in this lesson at least, each mode has a functional specialism. For example, the image provided a stable foundation on which to overlay, through speech and gesture, transient representations of movement and change. Other functions include the use of gesture to animate and locate; the use of material models to mediate the actual and the analysed; the use of (schematic) diagrams to abstract away detail; the use of the body to relate scientific knowledge to the here and now. Similarly, textual cohesion can be achieved through repetition, rhythm and parallelism of action, posture, and intonation. The affordances and constraints of the different modes help the communicator to decide what will be selected to do what. This selection of mode also makes meaning – for example, to choose gesture rather than words is to focus on physical movement rather than on movement lexically represented. The metaphorical path will be different in each case. Thus, throughout the series of lessons we suggest that each mode played a different part in the construction of the entity 'the human body'. Each mode required the students to do a different type of work in order to understand.

Finally, this multimodal analysis of communication in the science classroom raises a more general question: Is all this special to science? The answer is both yes and no. No because all communication is multimodal. Yes because science education makes some aspects much more salient than other school subjects – especially the combined emphasis on abstraction and analysis, the use of images for representation of knowledge (not as mere illustration), the connection with action through experiment and demonstration, and the overriding importance of material things in relation to words.

3

Analysing action in the science classroom

Introduction

Action is a highly theorized aspect of social interaction; nonetheless, it remains a relatively neglected source of data within educational research. This chapter attempts to highlight the significance of the analysis of organized action in education and in educational research. The importance of action in school science is firmly rooted in the history of science education and more generally in the history of science. It is also embedded in the (English) National Curriculum and the Nuffield Curriculum Projects over the last three decades, which have emphasized the importance of practical work in school science. In addition, within teacher training, inappropriate body language is generally recognized as a noticeable characteristic of ineffective teaching styles. However, as we keep on insisting, educational research has tended to focus on teaching and learning as a primarily linguistic accomplishment. We suggest that although action is recognized as important in some spheres it remains relatively under-theorized in the domain of teaching and of learning. The majority of methods developed to analyse action are idiosyncratic or focus on behaviourist and pyschologistic approaches. In our opinion, such approaches often fail to address the social aspects of meaning-making, are difficult to apply to the context of education, and are often not appropriate to the questions raised by the research context.

This chapter describes and demonstrates an analytical approach to action applicable to the classroom. It draws on social semiotic theories of meaning-making and Vygotsky's (1986) theories of mediated activity in order to comment on the complex relationship between the semiotics of social action and the situated experience of learning in the classroom. We describe the application of the schema to two case-study examples and explore how action realizes meanings and shapes classroom interaction. The first example explores the ways in which gesture can be used to make apparent and classify the usually invisible through the use of pantomimic gesture and demonstration of the imaginary, in this case the classification of states of matter (gas, liquid and solid) in a lesson with Year 9 students. The second example takes a detailed look at some students' use of experimentation (routinized action), focusing on their manipulation of objects and their construction of themselves as learners.

In conclusion we draw attention to the pedagogical implications of focusing on action in the science classroom and education more generally, and make some comments on implications for research in education and for communication more generally. We demonstrate that action is a semiotically well-articulated mode that has a greater communicative range than the interpersonal alone.

A focus on action

We view action and other modes of communication as realizing many different functions in social activity – to communicate about the world, to form and express relationships between people and to create coherent texts. We see action, speech and writing as distinct modes, each of which offers particular options of choices, affordances and constraints for meaning-making (Kendon, 1996; Lemke, 2000).

We use action as a broad term to encompass different forms. Gesture generally refers to the combined use of the face, arms and hands in motion and is usually associated with the expression of emotion or symbolic meanings which elaborate on or extend verbal messages. We focus on a range of gestures within the classroom including those that refer explicitly to objects (usually described as iconic, metaphoric or symbolic) and the use of gestures to 'punctuate' the text (usually referred to as beats). We also explore the movement of the body, of body posture and position, and the body and use of space as meaning-making resources: we might say, gesture with the whole body (Merleau-Ponty, 1969; Crowder, 1996). The science classroom involves teachers and students in meaningful manipulation of models and equipment, the exhibition of objects, and the use of demonstration and experiment. For this reason we include the manipulation of objects within our discussion of action, including the manipulation of imagined objects or entities through pantomimic gesture.

Our interest is the interpretation of action as a meaning-making resource within the classroom, and we view it therefore as the choices teachers and students make, rather than simply their 'behaviour'. In short, what we mean by *action* is *behaviour based on meaning* and the *act* is *action in a social context.*

Communication in the science classroom is a multimodal event in which action as mode is one thread in a complex weave of communicative action. We do not view action as generated by language, that is, we do not see gesture as a 'lexical' or other support generated by and for language. However, at times it may be that, just as speech may be generated by action. We propose what has been called a 'syncretic model' of speech, writing, gesture and thought, resulting in an interactive interface between language and gesture (McNeil, 1992). In this model, action has an active role in thought, where thought is taken as 'coming into existence with' and not only *expressed in* words, actions or images (Crowder, 1996). We view all communicative modes as mediating thought, where thought is both expressed and transformed in its representations in speech, writing, activity and visual modes; that is, in its multimodal realization. In this way gesture and other forms of action are central to communication and learning.

In viewing communication in the science classroom as involving images, action, writing and speech – a multimodal event – we are concerned not with identifying the order or rank of importance of modes (i.e. the usually dominant question of whether gesture is dependent on speech, etc.) but with the characteristics of the complex interrelation of action, linguistic resources and the visual. Whether actions are central or adjunct to speech, they work together with all other modes to realize meaning. Our interest is in the affordances and constraints of different modes and on the ways in which the affordances of action contribute to the meaning-making process (see also Martinec, 1997; Franks and Jewitt, 2001; Wells, 2000).

So to clarify our stance, we are not arguing here that speech, writing and action are necessarily of *equal* importance in all meaning-making processes, but that *they are all important aspects of meaning-making and therefore demand our attention.* In our attempt to get at the meaning of action we explore the meaning-making structures of action. We draw on the idea of grammar as a semiotic resource for encoding interpretations of experience and forms of social action, rather than as a formal rule system isolated from meaning (Halliday, 1985).

Action as a mode of communication is generally held to be less articulated than language and to convey meaning differently. The degree to which action as a meaning system, a mode, is articulated varies. In the case of gesture and sign languages, gesture is a fully articulated means of communication. In the science classroom gesture and action are less fully articulated than are the linguistic resources and gesture is only one of several modes of communication in operation. Gesture in the science classroom can be likened to a language system which is weakly lexicalized in that each lexical item is potentially vaguer, broader and more open to wider use as a signifier in new signs. Unlike in the English or mathematics classroom, students' use of action in the science classroom is an expected mode of communication. Gestures in particular can reveal knowledge not realized in verbal communication and they figure crucially in the construction, as well as the communication, of scientific insights (Crowder, 1996).

Our aim is not to identify 'universal meanings' but to map the role of action in the learning and teaching of science in the classrooms we observed and to draw some tentative generalizations about the role of action in science education.

Analysing action

A detailed explanation of our approach to action without reference to case-study examples would reduce it to a relatively unilluminating inventory of terms. For this reason a detailed description of our approach is integrated with the analysis of action later in this chapter. Five themes which emerged from our review of the literature had a significant influence on our analysis of action – the boundaries of space and time; the body; the objects and artefacts which mediate action; the notion of frame; and the 'grammar' of action.

Our approach to the analysis of action is a synthesis of ideas and approaches from psychology, sociology, anthropology and linguistics, in order to develop an approach that reflects the complexity of action and the interconnectedness of 'mind' semiosis, the social and the historical. Our anchor in this interdisciplinary approach is the desire to understand meaning-making and learning as a social and dialogic process expressed through the choices and driven by the motivations and interests of individuals who are located within the cultural domains that bind those choices. We have moved away from descriptive classifications and taxonomies of action (e.g. Ekman and Friesen, 1969; Efron, 1972; Freedman, 1972) to focus on the social function of actions served, on action as mode, and on how action interacted with the other modes of communication operating in the context of the classroom. Starting with the question 'What is the function of action in communication?', our analysis generated semiotically motivated classifications of meaning-potentials.

Our data is primarily in the form of video recordings of science lessons.[1] We classified the video recordings of classroom interaction into discrete units for analysis by applying the notion of (rhetorical) frame. We identified gross shifts in posture, position, communicative mode and content as indicators of frame/unit (Scheflen, 1973, 1974; Bateson, 1987). This chapter focuses on a sample of units in which action appeared to be significant in being foregrounded.

As described earlier, we built up a detailed description of the data, by viewing these tapes many times: with image only, with sound only, and with both sound and image. Through intensive group viewing of the data using the concept of frame, we built a description of classroom interactions (the transcription process focused on all modes: of action, speech and the visual). We produced a systematic account of action

---

[1] These data are supplemented by four other sources: observation notes made during the lesson; materials used in the lesson (e.g. textbooks, worksheets); texts produced by pupils and teacher; video and transcripts of focus groups with pupils.

from descriptive dimensions highlighted as important in the literature: eye movement, direction and gaze, facial expression, hand and arm movement/configurations, the use of the whole body to make gestures, body posture, the position of people in the room and their use of space, the location and context of the action (e.g. the semiotics of architecture), and the semiotic objects of action. In short, a 'thick descriptive' account was produced to show how actional, visual, and linguistic resources work together to make meanings.

We analysed this account to explore how action realized different meanings and to classify the ways in which it was used to represent what was going on (Halliday's (1985) ideational meaning); how action brought about interactions and relations between teachers and students (interpersonal meaning); and how action by itself and with the other modes formed meaningful communicative texts (textual meaning). Textual meanings were realized in many ways through action, for example, through the teacher's move from the back of the classroom – where she had been reading aloud from the whiteboard – to the front of the room, the raised podium behind the bench, thus marking the transition from one textual unit (rhetorical frame) to the next. Through this classification process we generated functionally motivated classifications of action.

We examined the patterns and structures of action, to understand the meaning structures and the ways these were combined to make meaning through action. In order to do this we focused on aspects of action in four main ways. First, we explored the role of different semiotic objects in action: what types of things were manipulated and how the teacher's and the students' interaction with these objects brought them into existence or momentarily transformed them. Second, we looked at action in relation to the other modes operating in the classroom. Through examining the cooccuring modes and viewing actions across the lesson we identified repetitions, reiterations and transformations of action. Through this comparison of incidence we were able to identify what Scheflen (1974) calls customary acts: acts that happen in a particular context at a particular time, and which have an established functional meaning. Third, we contrasted the tension between modes, for example, what was said verbally and what was performed through action. Why might action have been introduced at a particular point in a lesson? What did it enable the teacher or student to do? Through this process of comparison and contrast we attempted to unpick the role of action in the communicative event viewed holistically. Fourth, we examined the context of the action to identify the functional meaning of the action in relation to larger units of communication (e.g. Did the action open up the dialogue, or manage the transition from one type of speech to another?). Viewing of the synchronized video tapes of teacher and student activity enabled us to explore the dialogic and collaborative nature of action in the science classroom. Through the comparison of actions, modes and contexts we identified repetitions, reiterations, structured patterns and transformations of action. Below we summarize the ways that some actions have become conventionalized.

Conventionalized forms of action in the science classroom

Our analysis of examples of action in the science classroom suggests that some actions have solidified into conventionalized forms such as imaginary demonstration, demonstration with or on material objects, visual display or exhibition, experiment and investigation, and analogy. Each of these conventionalized forms appeared to be mediated by different objects and to realize some particular rhetorical functions.

Imaginary demonstration

We refer to a demonstration where an entity is brought into existence through action with the body, such as pantomimic gesture, where the body itself acts as a rhetorical sign. Imaginary demonstration was used across the range of science lessons to make apparent particular entities which are usually unseen (e.g. microbes, blood circulation, the universe), theoretical entities such as orbits, and historical aspects of entities (e.g. the life history of a star). In this way the teacher's imaginary demonstrations drew on the students' experience of the everyday world to rhetorically reconceptualize it. Our analysis in example one includes a detailed discussion of the communicative role of imaginary demonstration.

Demonstration

During the demonstrations we observed how the teacher interacted with scientific equipment and stood at the front of the class behind the bench. The authoritative position of the teacher in the room and the authority imbued in the equipment through its history and specialist nature were part of a rhetorical strategy used to make scientific ideas that are often counter-intuitive appear more plausible. Unlike interaction with everyday objects where the rhetorical framing appeared to function to *connect* the everyday and the scientific, the rhetorical framing of interaction with scientific objects in the context of a demonstration was the construction of scientific fact and of authority as *distinct* from the everyday. The role of mediating objects in demonstration is discussed in our analysis of example one.

Experiment

Experiment and investigation involved the students and teacher in interacting with both everyday and scientific objects. Experiment realized the rhetorical function of constructing science as collaborative exploration and constructing the students as 'scientists' through being brought into the habitus of science via the handling of the equipment (e.g. microscope, stethoscope). Experiment also rhetorically transformed the everyday into the realm of the scientific (e.g. the transformation of an 'onion' into a 'collection of cells' discussed in Chapter 5). Experiment was used to construct entities (e.g. the valves of the heart, energy, states of matter) and 'fact' through empirical evidence and the rhetorical stance of 'see/do it for yourself'. In this way experiment realized and construed a realist approach to the nature of science. The role of experiment in the construction of fact and the experience of doing science in the classroom is an aspect of our analysis in example two.

Analogy

Teachers and students drew on the behaviour and movement of a range of everyday objects and phenomena (e.g. one-way road systems, road works and plumbing) to make analogies through gesture and in their interaction with models. Through this process the socio-cultural and socio-historical meanings of the everyday object were brought into the science classroom as another meaning-making resource. For instance, in order to explain the cause of a heart attack a teacher drew an analogy between the arteries of the heart and a kitchen sink. He described how when he cooked he did not always bother to strain the rice properly, resulting in 'blocked pipes'. Through this analogy a heart attack was clearly linked with food and associated with individual carelessness. The analogical connections made with the visible everyday world appeared to be a way of asserting the realism of scientific truth. We observed that analogy in the science classroom tended to concern two key concepts in science education: spatial relationships (containment) and directionality. Analogy through action is discussed in detail in our analysis of example one.

Visual display through action

Here we refer to the interconnectedness of the visual and the actional in the production of an image, that is, where the action of producing the image is as important as the image produced. For example, in a lesson on energy the teacher gave the students a set of images on cards which depicted a 'job' and a 'source' of fuel (e.g. a match and a melting ice cube). The task was to match the job with the source. The iterative action of pairing, discussion and re-pairing enabled by the action with the cards was key to the task. Visual display through action tended to realize the rhetorical framing of science as establishing fact and certainty through a process of classification. In general, this process involved the students in rhetorically 'rubbing out differences' between everyday entities in order to reconceptualize the world. This is discussed in the context of regularized shapes of knowledge in Chapter 4.

Objects which mediate action in the science classroom

The actions in the science classrooms we observed were mediated by a range of objects which can crudely be described as either everyday or scientific. We argue that these two types express different socio-cultural and socio-historical meanings and semiotic potentials, the expression of which influenced the ways in which teachers and students interacted with them to make meanings.

Everyday objects (e.g. an onion, sand, cotton buds) were brought into the classroom and through the physical/conceptual (re)framing of the classroom, and their handling in a scientific procedure, they were (for that moment) transformed. In short, the rhetorical framing of the science classroom brought forth new expressions from the material objects – an onion became a collection of cells, sand became a solid, cotton buds became an implement for collecting unseen microbes. The familiar was temporarily transformed into the unfamiliar. Through the reframing of the everyday the students came to see new qualities and functions in entities and to see the scientific potential within the everyday. The everyday world thus temporally entered the scientific. Scientific objects (e.g. Newton Meter, models, microscope, Petri dishes) did not have a meaning for the majority of the students outside of the science classroom. They expressed 'science' and the history of science (they did not express the future of science). Their value was heightened by the way they were introduced and handled by the teacher and their rarity in the classroom. Scientific objects, unlike everyday objects, were specifically designed to express scientific meanings, and interaction with them imbued the actions of students and teachers with 'scientificness'.

We observed how teacher and student interaction with everyday and scientific objects shaped different rhetorical meanings, which in turn fashioned the interaction itself. Action with everyday objects tended to realize two types of rhetorical framing. First, those which presented everyday experience as *central* to scientific knowledge and understanding, through the rhetorical stance of 'you know this is true' (i.e. based on your experiences of the everyday), of science as direct experience and exploration, and the establishment of fact and certainty through simplicity and personification. Second, those which used strong references to the everyday but placed it *outside* of scientific knowledge and understanding through the rhetorical stance of reconceptualizing the world (by making the usually invisible visible or creating the need for explanation). Teacher and student interaction with scientific objects tended to realize rhetorical framing differently. Interaction with scientific objects presented the rhetorical possibilities of the science classroom in three main ways: first, the rhetorics of the science classroom as being a matter of fact and certainty through authority, empirical evidence and classification; second, the rhetorical stance of science as a fair and objective process of observation; third, the presentation of science as authoritative through its historical pedigree (e.g. narratives of Newton and gravity).

The construction of particles through actional modes

This example is drawn from the second lesson in a series of lessons on particles with Year 9 students. The topic of the lesson was 'states of matter'. Through this example we focus firstly on how the teacher's actions can bring entities (in this case 'particles') into existence, and secondly on how a teacher's actions can require students to reconceptualize the world, in this case through the reconstitution of everyday phenomena (solid, liquid and gas) through analogy and classification. Throughout our discussion we explore the interrelations between action and rhetoric. In particular we highlight the role of the teacher's body, of imaginary demonstration in the rhetorical characterization of the qualities of states of matter, and the use of analogy to reconceptualize the entities 'solid', 'liquid' and 'gas'.

The text in Figure 3.1 provided a context and starting point for the teacher's actions in the lesson. At times the text was made salient, at other times it was backgrounded, but throughout the lesson it provided a textual anchor for communicative acts of different kinds. Here, we offer a brief analysis of the meanings it realized in order to contextualize our analysis.

Several ideational meanings are realized visually by the text. First, each image has progressively fewer particles in it, while the particles remain the same size and shape. The difference between states of matter is represented as a question of how the particles are arranged, rather than of characteristics of the particles themselves. In this way the composition of the image suggests that a solid, a liquid and a gas are the same but 'have' different amounts of 'the same'. Second, the images of 'a solid', 'a liquid', and 'a gas' work as a series and highlight

There are three states of matter: solid, liquid and gas. We have found out that solids, liquids and gases are made of tiny particles. The difference between solids, liquids and gases is how the particles are arranged.

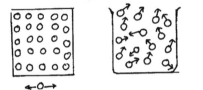

| In a solid, the particles are close together and vibrate about a fixed point. | In a liquid, the particles can move past each other, they can flow. | In a gas, the particles can move very fast and freely. They fill any space available. |

When a solid changes to a liquid, or a liquid changes to a gas or the other way round, we say there has been a change of state.

FIGURE 3.1 *Text on blackboard at the beginning of the lesson.*

that they have more in common with one another than may appear to be the case in our everyday experiences of them. For example, students' everyday knowledge and experience of sand, water and air most likely serves to make concrete for them their differences, while this image as a visual expression of their essence realizes their similarities. The image suggests that the three are of a kind, even though each is also represented as a distinct 'state of matter' framed and separated from the others. Third, the centrality of the image of a liquid serves to suggest that this state mediates the other states.

The writing beneath each image reads 'In a solid . . . In a liquid . . . In a gas . . .'. In this way the entities 'solid', 'liquid', and 'gas' have become 'containers' of particles. Our experience in the everyday world is one of interacting with the outer shell of the phenomenon 'particles'. The text realizes the difference to be explained in the lesson – it is not a matter of substance but a matter of movement, containment and of space.

The text provided the students with a resource to imagine with. Later in the lesson the teacher 'captures' air in her hand and then 'releases it'. Through her actions she asked the students to imagine the gas particles flying off and filling the room. The text on the blackboard provided some of the resources required to carry out this imaginative work – a concrete visualization of particles to think with. Later in the lesson the text provided a visual overlay which mediated the actions of the teacher and provided a visual link between the imagined particles in the text (as circles) and the physical substitute particles in the model (billiard balls). The constraints of the visual mode mean, however, that the image cannot readily realize the movement of the particles as shown by the fact that the teacher had to resort to the use of arrows and of cartoon symbols to indicate movement.

The body and imaginary demonstration

Focusing on action as a social rather than a biological phenomenon means understanding the body we act with (the material means of our action) in the same light. The social character of the body, social attitudes, traditions and techniques are assembled, transmitted and 'borrowed' through action, imitation and transformation: realized as *habitus* (Mauss, 1979). The expression of the body is shaped by the social order imposed by the environments and cultures we inhabit (Merleau-Ponty, 1969). In this way we suggest that the body is central to understanding the meaning of action. In this way, the process of action can be understood as 'bringing meaning into being' rather than as translating meaning into action. In other words we see the body as a meaning-making resource with which we produce signs, while the body is itself a sign. For example, the demeanour of the teacher's body when using a microscope can embody scientific, historical traditions and knowledge. A teacher's posture may indicate respect for the equipment, while the angle of the teacher's look may show his or her understanding of the effect of light on the mirrors, and the stillness of the teacher's body may itself embody 'observation': the act of 'doing being a scientist'. Students make sense of and learn the science teacher's *habitus* through their transformation of what they perceive as the teacher's bodily gesture.

The construction of the characteristics of gas particles

As the frame shifts from the teacher reading the text on the board to her imaginary demonstration, the teacher's action and her body became the canvas for the representation of particles. Standing at the back of the classroom, she clasped her hands together to 'capture' some air in her hands and began to walk slowly and carefully to the front of the classroom holding her clasped hands out in front of her body (transcript in Figure 3.2).

Her carefulness was exaggerated, and emphasized the existence and fragility of the gas in her hand. She stood at the front of the classroom facing the students, her body still and straight, her hands clasped and held out in front of her. She then sprung open her hands, dropped her left hand to her side and moved her right hand in two zig-zag waves in front of her as if to show the tracks of the released particles (transcript Figure 3.3).

The teacher's initial holding gesture coincided with her comment 'keep an amount of air' and marked the phrase 'in a small space' (Figure 3.2). These gestures were generated in this instance not wholly by convention. They exploited existing cultural meanings (such as the process of capturing, catching, holding, the hands as walls, the cupped and joined hands as a container) although the overall meaning was newly assembled. In another context these gestures may have meant something slightly different, i.e. their meaning was

T: If you've got a small space and you keep an amount of air in a small space . . .

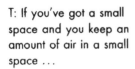

FIGURE 3.2 *Excerpt 1 from transcript.*

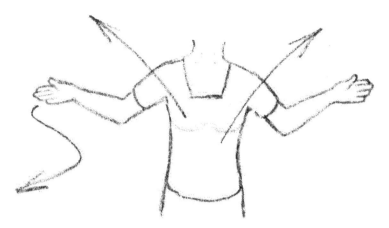

T: Say in my hand, I've got a certain amount of gas in my hand, OK, if I open my hand, then the particles that make up the gas, they go all over the place, they fill up the room, they move all around the room, OK?

FIGURE 3.3 *Excerpt 2 from transcript.*

situated – the gestural/actional lexis was not a given, but nor was it arbitrary. Although the teacher's gestures coincided with her speech, they did not simply correspond with its meaning, since her speech and her gesture were doing something different.

The teacher's actions realized the rhetorical construction of the entities and requested the students to see the world in a particular way through the representation, orientation and organization of meaning. First, her clasped hands provided the container for the invisible, bringing the unseen into sight. Her capturing action brought the mental visualization of particles into being, making them a tangible entity. Second, the way she quickly shaped her hands together suggested movement – if something wasn't moving it would not need to be 'captured'. Third, the delicate way in which she held her hands imbued gas/air with a butterfly-like ephemeral quality illustrating the instability of a gas. The teacher's actions orientated meaning in the everydayness that it located in people's relationship with air – it is there all around us, no special scientific equipment is required and anyone can reach out and hold it in their hands. At the same time, her shift in position to the front of the class was authoritative and her posture was declarative.

The teacher's sudden hand and arm movements contrasted with the stillness of the rest of her body and served to suggest that the particles, rather than herself, were the agent of the action. This was further suggested by the way she dropped her left hand to her side while her right hand represented a particle. Her actions suggested the speed and movement of the particles. The zigzag movements combined with her statement that 'they go all over the place' (Figure 3.3) to suggest the individuality of the particles' movement. Through the use of her body and imaginary demonstration she transformed the classroom from an empty static space to one full of moving particles. In effect the classroom became a container.

The construction of the characteristics of solid particles

Still standing at the front of the classroom and facing the students, the teacher repeated the demonstration with a solid. She swivelled around, picked up a piece of chalk, placed it in the palm of her right hand, cupped her left hand over the chalk and returned to face the class. She then took away her left hand and dropped it to her side (transcript Figure 3.4).

The teacher's casual arm and hand movement to demonstrate the movement of particles in a solid contrasted with the earlier sudden springing apart of her hands in demonstrating the behaviour of particles in a gas. In addition, the limpness of her body here contrasted with

T: If I do that to a solid, has it moved anywhere?
S: No.

FIGURE 3.4 *Excerpt 3 from transcript.*

its tautness then. Whereas she had used two hands to capture and release the gas, she used both hands to capture the solid but only moved one to release it. The materiality of the physical object that the teacher acted with (chalk) fashioned her actions. The contrast between her actions imbued the solid and the gas with different meanings. Her actions suggested that less force was needed to contain the particles in a solid than in a gas, that particles in a solid are less active (more stable) than those in a gas. In the previous lesson (which centred on compression) the solid used was sand, here it was chalk. Thus the rhetor's selection of entity is a rhetorical choice and the materiality of the solid can be seen as a rhetorical resource. If the choice of solid had been reversed neither demonstration would have worked. If sand had been used in the demonstration of particles, the answer to the teacher's question 'If I do that to a solid has it moved anywhere?' would have been 'Yes'. The same is true of the selection of equipment in the demonstration of the behaviour of particles in a liquid. The choice of material is a key rhetorical aspect of the construction of entities.

The construction of the characteristics of liquid particles

Still standing at the front of the classroom, the teacher used a squeezy bottle, a jug and water to demonstrate the behaviour of particles in a liquid. She squirted water from the bottle into the jug. She raised the bottle, simultaneously lowered the jug and swilled the water in the jug around in a circular motion. She then squirted more water into the jug, lowered the water bottle to the same level as the jug and continued to swirl around the water in the jug as she dropped her arm and the water bottle to her side. With the exception of her arm and hand movements, her body remained still. Through her stillness and her distancing of the bottle and jug from her torso she attempted to remove herself as agent from the process. This was reflected in her speech where the water ('it') became the agent (transcript Figure 3.5).

The demonstration relied on the interaction between the teacher's actions, her choice of equipment and the sample liquid. Had she waved about her arms as she squirted the bottle of water or used a water spray or a hose it would have 'gone all over the place'.

T: You can squeeze the
water, it flows, but does it
go all over, does it go all
over the, all over the place?

S: It drops.

T: Drops and it will take
up the shape of whichever
container I put it into.
Here it's in a bottle shape.
If I put it into this container,
OK, it's free to move but
it doesn't move all over
the room.

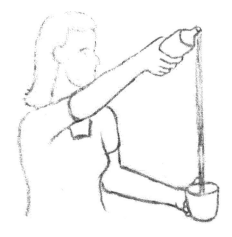

FIGURE 3.5 *Excerpt 4 from transcript.*

But there are no surprises: the demonstration was of a commonplace action providing a generalized backdrop to the mantra 'water takes the shape of the container'. The actions were emblematic representative behaviour, part of classification through which the construction of entities and a reconceptualizing of the world was realized.

Constructing difference

Through the teacher's actions the essential difference between a solid, a liquid and a gas was constructed as a difference in the tension between containment and freedom of movement. This concept was developed further through the teacher's action with a series of models and her use of analogy.

Reconceptualizing the world through interaction with models and analogy

The meaning of the objects and entities which mediate the learning of school science is materialized in our interactions with them in the science classroom and elsewhere. Meanings may be embodied

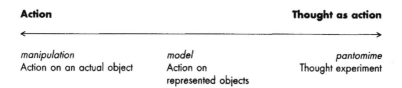

FIGURE 3.6 *Continuum of action.*

in objects themselves through historical human interaction with them. Through experiencing an object in a certain way it takes on a meaning beyond its materiality. Objects in the science classroom are framed by the science lesson and made suitable objects of scientific thought and experimentation through the activity of the teacher and students. Through this process an object acquires a new (if temporary and context-bound) 'form of existence' in the science classroom: *it acquires new significance.* In this way we suggest that scientific equipment shapes the potentials for meaning in the science classroom and interaction with equipment fashions meanings which in turn conventionalizes objects and promotes them into routinized scientific actions or 'ritual'.

We use the terms 'entity' and 'object' to include that which is brought into being through the imagination of teachers and students. We treat actions in the science classroom on a continuum of representation as in Figure 3.6 (Crowder, 1996).

Here we concentrate on how the teacher's action with the models of particles in a solid, a liquid and a gas constructs the entity 'particle' through its behaviour and reconceptualizes the world. In particular, we discuss the way the teacher constructs the concept of 'containment' differently in each state of matter.

Reconceptualizing the movement of particles in a solid

Standing behind the raised front bench the teacher picked up a model of particles in a solid (made of plastic balls and wire) and placed it on the centre of the bench. The teacher asked a student 'What does *vibrate* mean?' After some laughter a definition of *vibrate* was reached: 'backwards and forwards about a fixed point'. The teacher kept one hand on her hip, her body still, and with the other hand she

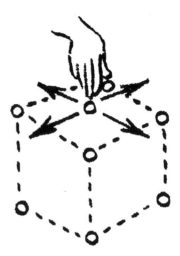

T: These are the particles and how they are arranged in a solid. It's a bit like jelly, they can move around a point, but do they move away?

Ss: No.

FIGURE 3.7 *Excerpt 5 from transcript.*

gently wobbled the model. Her actions were restrained. Her action with the model visually defined vibration (Figure 3.7).

The teacher then laid her hand lightly across the top of the model and drew an analogy between the movement of soldiers and the movement of the particles. She then lifted her hand and used both hands to represent the direction of the row of 'soldiers': she rolled her hands towards her body (backwards), then forwards, and finally to the side of her body. Then she patted the top of the model. The model moved. She held her hand flat on the model for a second and took it off. The model moved more slowly (Figure 3.8).

The model was a concrete physical metaphor for the particles in a solid, indeed the teacher referred to the model as 'the particles'. The action of the teacher with the model (mediational means) realized meanings about the particles in a solid in a number of ways. First it represented the materiality and shape of the particles: round and hard. Second, it represented their relationship to one another: structured, evenly spaced and connected to one another. Third, when the teacher flicked the model with her hand her action gave it expression. As she flicked she stepped back from the model physically distancing herself from the effect of her interaction with the model and imbuing it with agency. The continued movement of the model provided the context

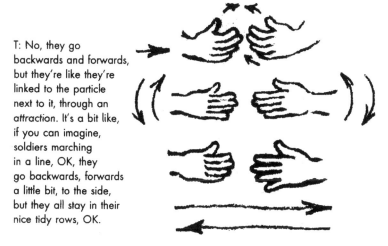

T: No, they go backwards and forwards, but they're like they're linked to the particle next to it, through an attraction. It's a bit like, if you can imagine, soldiers marching in a line, OK, they go backwards, forwards a little bit, to the side, but they all stay in their nice tidy rows, OK.

FIGURE 3.8 *Excerpt 6 from transcript.*

for her question to the students: '. . . they can move around a point, but do they move away?'

The teacher's action with the model realized the movement of the particles and provided the students with the physical evidence they needed to give a correct answer to her question 'Do they move away?'

It was the interaction between the material expression of the models and the teacher's action which constrained the movement of the particles. The teacher used a model to demonstrate a reality that the model had itself been designed to express. The model remained subject to the constraints of the world that the teacher was attempting to overcome – manipulating the substance was problematic, so, curiously, she had to *make happen* what she asserted *was happening.* The teacher needed to find a way to show that it was the model that moved rather than her who moved it. Her use of the model to convey the behaviour of particles was constrained by its materiality. The salience of the model was backgrounded as the teacher's hand carried the notion of rows from the model and used her hands to gesture the direction of the movement of the particles/ soldiers. Her action represented the action of soldiers as routinized and disciplined. Indeed she had to slow down the movement of the model (by placing her hand on the model, holding it for a second and then removing her hand) in order to do this. Through this action she returned to her body as a resource for meaning-making.

Analogy was one rhetorical resource the teacher chose in order to overcome the difficulty of conveying the motivated movement of the particles in the model. Analogy is the process of establishing a relationship, irrespective of mode. An analogical relationship can be between elements in one mode, or across modes. In the examples which follow, the teacher used language to describe the analogical relationships between the action of the models and the action of jelly wobbling, soldiers marching in a line, footballers playing on a pitch, and shoppers at the January sales. In this way she evoked the analogy linguistically, but the analogical relationship itself remained between the two forms of action brought into comparison: the movement of the model of a solid and the soldiers marching in a line; the movement of the balls in the model of a liquid and a gas and the behaviour of footballers or shoppers at the sales. Language was thus a means of drawing out the analogical relationship rather than itself being one of the analogical elements. The teacher's selection of jelly drew attention to the movement of the model and explained it in terms of the movement of a solid which can simultaneously hold the notion of wholeness, stability and movement. But the movement of jelly did not draw attention to, or account for, the presence and structure of the particles represented in the model.

The teacher's carrying/lifting action with the model grounded her gestural analogy firmly in the model. At the same time her action and the analogy transformed the structure of the model. Through her analogy the teacher attempted to remove the material links between the particles as presented in the model – to transform the plastic bonds which held together the particles in the model into psychological links of attraction and discipline: '. . . they're like they're linked to the particle next to it, through an attraction' (Figure 3.8).

When the teacher patted the top of the model she replicated the movement she had previously described in her speech and gesture: 'they all stay in their nice tidy rows'. The model realized its structure; the teacher's actions realized the *movement* of the patterned structure. The teacher's action with the model presented an idealized version of the everyday examples she had used earlier in her imaginary demonstration. It enabled the students to see what previously they had to imagine: the particles inside the outer shell of the sample solid. Indeed, the model was itself an idealized solid since it did not represent the molecular structure of a specific compound.

Reconceptualizing the movement of particles in a liquid

In order to exhibit the behaviour of particles in a liquid and a gas the teacher used a wooden tray containing a wooden slat and white hard plastic balls (as shown in Figure 3.9).

The teacher held the frame horizontally in front of her body. She used the left section of the model to represent the particles in a liquid. She flicked/plucked the balls in the model (Figure 3.10).

The teacher moved the balls in the frame. She developed the analogy with the movement of football players. She used her hands and arms and made circular movements away from her body in the horizontal plane to bring in the path of movement of the winger running around the top, passing the ball. Her actions showed the movement of each of the particles as interconnected and following directional and circular paths. The teacher used her finger to trace a rectangle horizontally in the air in front of the wooden frame of the model.

The teacher elaborated on the analogy of movement on a football pitch and the rules which govern this movement. She then repeated the action of drawing the 'pitch'. Through her actions the teacher reproduced the physical frame of the model as an imagined space. The analogy drew attention to the organized movement of particles/ players within a particular space and transformed the arena of this movement from a material/physical one to a human/imagined one. Thus she accounted for the difference between seen and unseen phenomena.

FIGURE 3.9 *Model of particles in a liquid.*

T: For a liquid, what I have to do is, I've got the particles, they're still quite close together but they can move around, OK, they're not in fixed lines like they are in the solid. It's a bit like, arr, a football team, OK ...

FIGURE 3.10 *Excerpt 7 from transcript.*

Reconceptualizing the movement of particles in a gas

The teacher removed five of the balls from the left side of the tray, placed them in the right side and turned the frame upwards by about 80 degrees to represent the particles in a gas.

The teacher held the model in front of her body and plucked the balls with her hands, moving them up the inside of the frame and letting them drop. She introduced an analogy between the action of the particles/balls and the frantic action of shoppers at the January sales. She continued to hold the model in front of her body and made six sudden gestures with her left arm, stretching her whole arm out and throwing it out from her body to the right, to above her head, and across her body to the left. (Each of these movements is marked* in the transcript Figure 3.11.)

As the teacher said 'the particles are moving very, very fast' she held one of the balls and moved it in a circle within the model. Her action showed the movement in space of these particles to be different. Her gestures represented the behaviour of the gas particles as motivated, directed and spinning, and at the same time sudden and unpredictable (to the extent that they dropped out of the model at one point). The teacher's gestures across the space of her upper torso showed gas particles to be all around her, whereas her gestures to represent the movement of the particles

T: All over the place, yeah, so one minute, soon as they're going through the door that's it,* someone goes over to the laundry section,* someone goes over to the, er, perfume counter,* someone goes to the TV section*, yeah, and as soon as they've grabbed* something they're off* to another department, so it's frantic, moving very very fast, the particles are moving very, very fast ...

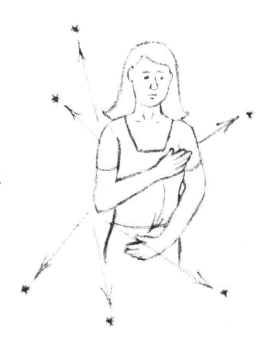

FIGURE 3.11 *Excerpt 8 from transcript.*

in a solid were confined to a smaller specified space. The teacher's representation of the behaviour of particles in a gas, in particular her grabbing as she stuck her hand out into the air, introduced the potential of particles to bond with one another – a behaviour also attended to in the analogy with the frenetic consumerism of shoppers at the January sales.

Summary

The teacher's movement of her body imbued certain qualities in different states of matter. In particular, her interaction with the models constructed the stability of solids, the transitory potential of liquids and the volatility of gases. Her actions represented the behaviour of particles in a gas, a liquid, and a solid as constrained in different ways and as having different relationships to space, with gas represented as less bound by the rules than either a liquid or a solid.

The teacher's action used different planes to represent each state of matter. The liquid particles were acted out within the horizontal plane – the liquid was swilled horizontally and the paths of particles in a liquid and the framing of the space they occupy in the model were represented horizontally. In contrast, the movement of gas particles was demonstrated in both instances (the paths of movement and the framing of the space the particles occupy) on the vertical plane.

The shift in the models used to represent a solid, a liquid and a gas signified that there is a similarity between a liquid and a gas that may not exist with a solid. In addition, the teacher's action with the model of the particles in a liquid and a gas realized the notion of containment and movement differently than her interaction with the model of the solid. The movement of particles was realized as a structured and a constrained event within a solid, constrained by the internal relationships between the particles. If one particle moved, they all moved. In the model of a liquid and a gas the teacher plucked individual balls and then used gesture to follow through the imagined movement of individual particles.

The different interrelations between space and freedom of movement embodied in the teacher's imaginary demonstration and use of models was echoed in her use of analogy. There was a shift in the analogies she used from the movement/behaviour of a group to that of individual action. First, the analogy for particles in a solid with the movement of a jelly, a homogenous lump, and marching soldiers in a line (a social group founded on the subjugation of the individual to the group). Second, the analogy between the movement of particles in a liquid and a football team where players have different roles and individuality. Third, the analogy of the movement of shoppers in the January sales, whose movement was based on their individualistic consumption and that of particles in a gas. The teacher's actions with the models of particles in a liquid and a gas characterized them as individuals within a collective. The teacher's choice of analogies imbued particles with agency through their personification as soldiers, football players and shoppers.

Through the teacher's action with the model and her use of analogy the notion of 'containment' was realized as the boundaries or rules of behaviour; an invisible constraint, rather than a purely physical space. In the case of liquid and the analogy with football, the majority of students probably either played, watched or had a knowledge of the game. Perhaps more importantly they know that many spaces can become a football pitch (a front room floor, a patch of grass, a street). A space becomes a football pitch by the behaviour we engage in within it and the rules we use to govern our behaviour. The students with an inside knowledge of football saw a pattern within the teacher's movement – the more intricate her movement, the more intricate the pattern – whereas those without this knowledge saw 'movement'. The teacher drew on their different knowledges, in particular the knowledge that rules affect behaviour. Her use of the football analogy can be seen as a demonstration of her 'entry' into the interests of the students. In this analogy, the particles represented as balls were transformed into football players and the wooden frame became 'field' – the space of movement. In this way, states of matter became a question of the tension between individual involvement and collective constraint within a given space.

Throughout the lesson the teacher's actions realized textual meaning through her mantra-like repetition of solid, liquid, gas. This occurred through the image, the text, the teacher's speech (five times), the demonstration and the use of analogy. This rhythm, combined with the teacher's pace of delivery as a mode, resulted in a sequential connection between the entities solid, liquid, gas: the pattern of her multimodal communicative acts created the rhythm and movement of particles. The form was not separate from the meaning the teacher was making. The form of the lesson was intrinsically woven into the content: it *was* the meaning. Through the form of the repetition liquid was always central, and in this way liquid was understood to mediate the process of change in states of matter as a state of transformation.

The entity 'particles' was constructed through the meaning created in the interweaving of the teacher's use of image, action, and speech (detailed in Table 3.1 below). This was not a purely linguistic accomplishment.

The different means (text, imaginary demonstration, model and analogy) presented different relationships to knowledge and required different types of work from the students engaged in the process of learning. The text presented a representation to imagine with. The teacher's imaginary demonstration showed the

Table 3.1 The meaning function of the teacher's image, action and speech

Meaning function	Visual	Action	Speech
Presentation of information (ideational)	Shape	Clasped hand: brought entity into existence	Named entities
	S, L, G are different amounts of 'the same thing'		Hypothesized (If I . . .)
	Visualized as a series: potential for change between states	Imbued qualities on particles: relation to containment stability – delicacy speed (release) motivation and agency movement (random collective)	Conferred entities with agency (They/It)
	Central position of liquid as mediator		Commentary
	S, L, G as containers	Provided physical 'evidence' answers ('translated' by students into speech e.g. 'do they move away?') – materiality	Questioned
	Set agenda: explanation needed is not a matter of substance but movement and containment		
		Emblematic representation (L: takes the shape of container)	Talking to create the idealized version (e.g. I act vs it acts – takes shape)

Definition (vibrate)	Model - materiality Structure/arrangement Agentive movement	Extended location of action (analogy – jelly, soldiers, footballers, sale shoppers)	
	'Pat' Replicates movement described in speech		
	Constructed difference	Signalled what to attend to (e.g. analogy and bonds)	
Orientation to audience (Interpersonal)	The 'depth' of science: looks inside the 'container' you experience in the everyday	Located teacher as source of info. - body	Constructed teacher as agent
		Made ideas 'seem' real - 'believe me'	Control
	A resource to think with - imagine with	A resource to think with - concretized	Vagueness - non-transactive actions
	Authority - given fact	Body distance - imbued objectivity	

(Continued)

Table 3.1 (Continued)

Meaning function	Visual	Action	Speech
		Authority model and shift to raised platform - control posture	
Organization (textual)	Anchor for meaning	Pace of mode Repetition Contrast	Pace of mode Repetition Contrast

S = solid, L = liquid, G = gas

movement and qualities of particles in different states of matter. Her use of analogy and models attempted to realize the structural relationships and movement of the particles so as to show the containment and the freedom of movement of particles in different states of matter.

The action of students in the science classroom: Burning fuels

The example discussed in this section is drawn from a Year 9 science lesson on energy and focuses on an investigation of what makes a good fuel. The investigation consisted of burning four types of fuel (metafuel tablets, paraffin, sawdust and paper), heating water in a boiling tube, and measuring and recording the highest temperature the water reached with each of the fuels. The teacher stood at the front of the classroom and delivered a monologue instructing the students on how to conduct the investigation. Her monologue, punctuated with the action of displaying the equipment to be used (the clock, tripod, etc.), served to translate a visual and written worksheet into action and speech. The teacher asked the students to work in groups of three or four and took a hands-off approach throughout the investigation. The analysis presented below demonstrates how students' actions can realize their involvement with the process of science in relation to two interconnected dimensions – the classroom as a space located in a particular time, and the semiotic objects which mediated the action in the classroom. Throughout we comment on the relationship between action and speech.

Position, space and time: The actional realization of roles

Time can be seen as a means for articulating temporal relations of 'before', 'after' and 'during'. Of course it also articulates socially shaped rhythms and relationships, the 'events' of social or personal histories. Space articulates relations, on the surface at least, such as 'in front of', 'inside', 'outside'. Space of course also articulates the present outcomes of social histories of power, values and knowledge which are realized in architecture, furnishings, allocations of space, etc. Context, the social-cultural analogue of space, articulates those shapings of social form and social practice over long periods of time (history) which are salient at this present moment of communicative action in particular settings and institutions.

Time and space can therefore be seen as dimensions or resources available to the meaning-maker via the creation of patterned structures of action (e.g. rhythm and pace). Students and teachers move in time through the space of the classroom, position themselves in relation to one another and to the artefacts of science – classroom interactions are located in a particular social space and a specific point in history. In short, time and space are distinct but interconnected dimensions which both articulate meanings and form a site of meaning-making. Human social behaviour is moulded by the cultural, social, and historical traditions in which it is produced – it is neither universal nor unique to individuals. The social use and arrangement of space (e.g. seating arrangements) in schools, in this case the science classroom, represent the petrified formalization of pedagogic power relationships (Sutton, 1992).

In this section we focus on how students' spatial positions and interactions played their part in realizing the rhetorics of 'doing science', and how this contributed to the process of making students see and feel themselves as learners within the science classroom. The activity which took place in the classroom was mediated by the layout of the classroom, the spatial relationships mapped out by the arrangement of the furniture (e.g. the students' benches and the raised teaching bench at the front of the classroom). To give a seemingly simple example, when working in small groups there was necessarily one student nearer the equipment than the others, who therefore potentially saw themselves as more peripheral to the investigation. Also, each group would be spatially isolated from the other which had consequences for the possibilities of (inter) action.

The transcript in Figure 3.12 describes the setting up of the investigation. The students collected the remaining equipment and sample fuels. The wooden clamp-stand was exchanged for a metal

Time	Action	Verbal
11.13	Ab: left the bench and returned with a Bunsen burner, a heat mat, safety glasses and a pair of tongs. He then left. A: stood up, walked around the bench, picked up the worksheet, placed the Bunsen burner on the mat. S: left the table, returned with a tripod. Ab: returned with a heat mat. A: put the Bunsen burner under the tripod and on top of the mat. Ab: put the heat tray on the tripod. S: left the bench. Ab: left the bench. A: moved the arrangement of equipment across the bench and connected the Bunsen burner to the gas outlet.	
11.14	Ab: returned with a clamp-stand and left. A: set up the clamp. S: returned with the stop-clock and put it on the table.	A: Abdul, go and get a test tube. Abdul, go and get a boiling tube.
11.15	A: put on safety glasses, looked at the work sheet and moved each piece of equipment, 'fine tuned' the set-up. Ab: left and returned with a boiling tube. Al: put the boiling tube in the top clamp. Ab: pointed at bottom clamp, moved around him to help take it out and put it in the bottom clamp. Ab: left the bench. A: set up the clamp and gave the boiling tube to Sadik.	Ab: Put this one there. Now we need something else to hold it there. A: Here. Hold this.
11.16	S: handed back the boiling tube. Ab: returned with a thermometer, handed it to Sadik, who looked at it and then placed it on the bench near Alamin. A: picked up the thermometer, put it in top clamp. Ab: stood next to Alamin and held it A: tightened the clamp.	

FIGURE 3.12 *Excerpt 1 from transcript.*

one. Alamin experienced considerable difficulty in fixing the clamps to the clamp-stand (as they were not compatible). Different clamps were fetched and tried. Eventually Alamin left the bench to collect the exercise books and draw up a results table. Abdul left to look for new clamps. Meanwhile Foysol and Sadik attempted to construct the equipment for the experiment. Abdul returned with another clamp and he and Sadik tried alternative ways of holding the thermometer. Alamin then returned to the task of setting up the equipment and demanded that Abdul find another clamp. Abdul returned with the correct clamp and together they set up the stand.

Although the students spoke during the task, our analysis shows that it was not their speech which organized the activity overall (see Table 3.2). The construal of meaning depended on the action process. In other words, the students realized (and construed) meaning through their actions. In particular the social and practical interrelations of students were realized through their spatial relationship to one another, their position and their interaction with the equipment during the setting up of the investigation.

The students' articulation of space through their repeated movements realized their involvement in the process of the doing of science. If one imagined a circle with a diameter of a metre with the equipment at its centre, this space could be a measure of the students' different 'involvement'. Alamin took a central position within this space of involvement. Throughout the setting up of the equipment Alamin was the central coordinator of the activity in the group. He did not move around the table until the equipment arrived. He rarely left the table to collect equipment (in contrast Abdul left and returned a total of 16 times). He placed each piece of equipment in position. He decided where on the bench the experiment took place.

Alamin connected the equipment (including the material frame for the investigation), measured the water, checked and counted the fuels, and drew the table for the results to be entered into (which the rest of the group later copied). His central position was realized and enforced through his position and the repetition of his actions and those of the other students. Abdul moved in and out of a near-central role, which was based on his movement through the classroom to collect equipment. Sadik and Foysol remained primarily on the edges of the investigation, literally 'hovering' on the margins. They entered the space of involvement to pass objects and when it was vacated by Alamin or Abdul, but primarily their role was that of observers.

Table 3.2 The type of meaning function realized in the students' action and speech

Type of meaning function realized	Mode	
	Action	Speech
Interpersonal	Roles in group (connector or collector) Dialogue - hierarchy Correction	Roles in group Monitoring
Ideational	Identification of resources, the connection of parts to make new things – realize new potentials – new meaning structures (arena) for action to happen in, attention to detail and order Marks the concepts of time and measurement	Identify gaps in equipment set-up to enable action to proceed
Textual	Establishes patterns of meaning in science process	

The students' positions worked to construe the collaborative yet hierarchical nature of science.

The students' actions, movement and position were the dominant semiotic mode in the setting up of the investigation. Their speech served to confirm their roles in the group: Alamin spoke more than the others, gave instructions and conferred with the teacher, while Abdul responded and monitored what was needed to enable the action to proceed. As summarized in Table 3.2, the students' action and speech realized different meanings and had different *functional specialisms*. On an interpersonal level, the students' actions realized their different roles in the task (as collectors, connectors and observers), their centrality to the task of doing science, and their position in the hierarchy of the group within the science classroom.

The students' actions realized ideational meaning through the collaborative construction of the material structure of the investigation: the arena of events to come, i.e. the arena of the investigation was not ready-made but was a system built with and structured from ready made parts. Throughout the setting up of the equipment the students worked to (re)produce the image on the worksheet with the resources available to them. Through action they redrew the worksheet as a three-dimensional physical entity. Here the worksheet image functioned as a spatial template anchor for the task and the students' actions. When Alamin looked at the worksheet and then realigned each piece of the equipment he attempted to reproduce the effect represented in the image. In this way the students' movements can be seen as the collaborative realization of the affect of science as a neat arrangement – the 'doing of science'.

That the students corrected one another via action rather than via speech shows that their actions served to realize the norms, order and structures of doing science. Through their actions the students identified the resources (the connection of parts) in order to make new meaning structures in which their future actions could have a place, and with which the meaning structures could happen.

Action, entities and objects:
The experience of being a learner

As stated earlier, the meaning of the objects and entities which mediate the learning of school science is materialized in our interactions with them in the science classroom and elsewhere. During the setting up of the investigation there was a shortage of the correct clamps and a range of incompatible clamps had been put out. Two of the students in the group (Foysol and Sadik) used the incompatible clamps and in so doing became engaged in an attempt to transform the set-up of the investigation by creating an alternative workable version. Their efforts focused on how to hold the thermometer in place. In this case, the process of setting up the investigation was constrained by the means which mediated it: the incompatible clamps. In this way the students' actions realized science as a structured and systematic process which could not be transformed.

Students' interactions with school science equipment contribute on the one hand to the classroom process of making knowledge, and on the other hand to their different experiences of being a learner in the science classroom. In this example Alamin and Abdul became part of the experiment through their handling of the equipment: they became 'proficient learners'. Their actions confirmed the learning value of doing it for yourself within school science. In contrast, Foysol and Sadik did not possess a viable tool (the correct clamp and a visual anchor within the worksheet) to mediate their action and their actions confirmed their lack of expertise within the science classroom. The students' interaction with the equipment framed the experiment by producing a physical structure, within which to communicate that embodied the constraints and affordances (the expression) of the material objects it was constructed from. In addition, this frame mediated the students' different expressions of 'becoming' scientific selves.

The next stage of the investigation – the burning of the four sample fuels – emphasized the role of objects in mediating action and the functional specialization of different modes. The students' actions with the equipment functioned to construct fact through empirical evidence. The first phase of the investigation – the burning of a sample of meta-fuel – is transcribed in Figure 3.13.

Here we suggest that different meanings were realized through the students' action and speech – action was the stuff of meaning, while speech provided the commentary on the detail of the action. As Table 3.3 suggests, action and speech were equally dominant in the meaning-making process detailed above, but were functionally different.

Throughout, the students' contact with the equipment suggested different levels of involvement with the investigation. Alamin handled a range of items (clock, clamp, boiling tube and fuel) and completed the results table. Abdul worked with a more limited range (he lit the

Time	Action	Speech
11.31	Ab: lights fuel with Bunsen. A: picks up clock and sets it. A: holds hands together as if holding fuel with tongs.	A: Am I supposed to keep on holding it like that? Ab: No, I don't think so.
	A: leaves bench.	A: I'm going to go and ask Miss.
	F: picks up worksheet and reads.	T: No. Once it's lit then that's all right. Ab: See!
	A: returns, lowers bottom clamp. S: points with his glasses at the experiment.	A: Make it a bit more lower. S: Check the temperature.
		F: It's about 30.
	A: points at Abdul.	A: Keep an eye on the temperature.
	All look at equipment. Ab: looks at thermometer, raises his fist,	Ab: It's going up, 31 yeah, 36, 39, 41,
11.32	starts to dance. A: checks clock.	50, 51, 52. A: Going to hold it for three minutes.
	Ab: puts his glasses on, leans in. A: gets his exercise book,	Ab: 61, 2, 3, 4, 5. A: I'll write the results down, yeah? Ab: OK.
	points at table, looks at Abdul.	A: Am I supposed to tick it? Name of sample tested. What's the sample? Ab: Thingy, energy cube.
	A: leaves table.	A: Miss? A: Tablet solid. S: Fuel solid.
	F: brings back box and gives it to A.	A: Meta-fuel they call it. Ab: No, solid fuel tablet. A: Meta-fuel.
11.33	T: arrives, holds box, reads. A: writes, reads table, looks at experiment, writes, reads table in exercise book, bends down, looks at experiment looks at Abdul, writes,	T: Meta-fuel. A: Easy to ignite? Ab: Yes. A: Does it keep burning? Yeah. Is there smoke? Abdul can you see any smoke?

FIGURE 3.13 *Excerpt 2 from transcript.*

fuel with the Bunsen burner and handled the clock). In contrast, neither Foysol nor Sadik physically interacted with any of the equipment during the first trial of the experiment. The students' roles within the

Time	Action	Speech
	looks at equipment. Ab: puts splint in flame, picks up clock.	Ab: No, there's only a flame. A: Abdul, leave it, Abdul, leave it. A: Oh, we leave it for 4 minutes, oh it's quite burning now. It's nearly 3 minutes. We're supposed to leave it burning now 'til it stops.
11.34	Ab: walks around, looks, takes glasses off, looks at thermometer. All lean forward and look. F looks at thermometer.	Ab: What is it? What is it? F: It's over 100. S: Leave it. A: Leave it until it stops burning.
	All leaning forward, looking. T picks up spare clamps	Ab: See how long it takes, innit? A: What? Ab: See how long it takes, innit? T: How are you doing boys, do you need these? Ab: See how long it takes to turn to ashes. T: It's boiling. You've finished. You've got too much mata-fuel there.
11.35	A: amends table, adds time column.	A: Ah wait, let me do another table. Tell me when it stops, yeah.

FIGURE 3.13 *(Continued)*

group which were apparent through their actions were also realized in their speech. Alamin gave the most instructions and only he made direct statements or asked questions. Abdul responded to most of these questions whereas Foysol responded to Sadik.

The students' interaction with the equipment and objects in the science classroom realized the construction of fact through empirical evidence, measurement and classification. The thermometer transformed the concept of heat into a materially quantifiable thing – a rise in the fluid in a thermometer – and in this way the factual evidence was made convincing. Through the ontological and epistemological understanding implicit in the investigation into what is a good fuel, the nature of science was constructed as reality. Scientific truth was achieved through the

Table 3.3 The meaning functions of students' use of action and speech

Type of meaning function realized	Mode	
	Action	Speech

Interpersonal	We are ready
	Roles in group:
	    establish authority,
	    involvement, excitement,
	    control, attention
		Teacher's authority
		Roles in group

Ideational	Indicates object of interest
	Process of observation
	Measurement
	Preparation
	Mediates definition
	Dialogue of verification
	Emphasizes area of
	    negotiation (e.g. holds
	    clock when negotiating
	    time with a group)
	Introduces alternative
	    agendas - students'
	    interests
		Refinement of actions
		Results of measurement
		Classification
		Definition
		Negotiation
		Instruction

Textual	Establishes patterns of
	    meaning in science
	    process: observe,
	    measure, record	

description of a visible, quantifiable measurement of 'reality'. The investigation created a direct relationship between scientific empirical data and reality.

The repetition of the students' actions throughout each phase of the investigation produced a contrast in time and space which itself realized meaning. Each phase of the investigation (each sample fuel) took a different length of time, and was performed with varying degrees of ease. The rhythm of the students' actions across the investigation was itself a form of (temporal) comparison which contributed to the construction of fact. The textual structure of the results table mediated the transformation of the students' repetitive actions (for the burning of each fuel) into comparisons of the characteristics of the fuels.

Our analysis suggests that students' interests and motivations are a key aspect in their action in the science classroom. For example, Alamin's interests informed his actions in response to the construction of what to do in the worksheet which stipulated the arrangement of the equipment, the process of repetition and the orchestration of the action. The worksheet included three images (Figure 3.14) with a strong diagonal vector (an angled line connecting elements in a visual composition, and suggesting action and interaction between them) acting on the fuel sample. The vector in the first image is formed by a Bunsen burner, in the second by a pipette, and in the third by a lit splint. Alamin attempted to 'translate' the action of the visual vectors through his action: He held his hands together 'as if holding fuel with tongs'. 'Am I supposed to keep on holding it like that?' (Figure 3.13). Through this action Alamin 'filled in' the human actor absent in the worksheet image.

The students' reading of the table on the worksheet provides another example of how resources made available by teachers in science lessons can mediate the activity of the students, and how students' interests can transform the meaning of teachers' instructions. The results table in the worksheet set the criteria for 'what is a good fuel' and provided a template for the students. Alamin copied the example table on the worksheet into his exercise book. In the extract at Figure 3.13 he used the table in order to understand what data was to be collected. Throughout, the students were uncertain what signified the end of the experiment: was it when the water boiled or reached its highest temperature, or when the fuel burnt out? The teacher's declarative, 'It's boiling. You've finished' confirmed that (at least in her view) it was the former. However, Alamin amended the table adding a column for time, indicating that for him the end was *also* when the fuel burnt out. This addition to the table enabled his interest in what makes a good fuel to be incorporated and transformed the text (the results table). In so doing, he transformed the purpose of the investigation

and the value 'good' shifted from the measurement of temperature
to the measurement of time (which we suggest could be a more
valid everyday criteria for Alamin in thinking about what makes a
good fuel).

What makes a good fuel?

Many things burn, but they do not all necessarily make good fuels. In this investigation you will burn
a variety of substances and try to decide which of them could be used as fuels for home heating.

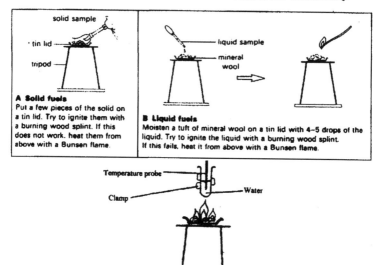

Once the fuel has ignited, place the boiling tube over the flame. Hold it in place with a clamp. Some
water and the temperature probe should be in the boiling tube.
Record your results in a table like the one below:

Sample tested	Is it easy to ignite?	Does it keep burning?	Is there only a little smoke?	Final temp (degrees C)	Does it leave only a little ash?

Now think about some of the other factors which may affect the usefulness
of each fuel. Is it natural or synthetic? Is it expensive or cheap? Can it be
transported easily and safely? Can it be stored safely? Are there better uses for
the material other than burning it as a fuel?

FIGURE 3.14 *The worksheet used in the lesson.*

The pedagogic implications of action as a meaning-making resource

The framework presented and exemplified in this chapter offers a way to address the social aspects of meaning-making applicable to education, in particular the ways in which students make and re-make signs across communicative modes in the processes of their learning. We have begun to assemble evidence to show that the communicative power of action is not restricted to particular science topics, nor does it exist within the realms of demonstration and experiment alone. Indeed we have shown how teachers and students made meaning through their position in the classroom, body posture, movement and their interaction with resources in the classroom.

In particular, our analysis of action demonstrates that action communicates meaning and shapes interaction in the classroom in many different ways. Action in the science classroom can bring entities into existence, imbue them with certain qualities and confer agency. It can challenge our conceptions of the world and provide us with resources to imagine and think with. Action can make ideas seem real, create involvement, construct fact and convey the realism of scientific truth. It can bring forth different expressions of self as learner or teacher and connect the worlds of science and the everyday in concrete ways, connecting disparate areas of knowledge to make new meanings. It can convey social responsibilities, express historical meanings and the experiences of science. Through action something can be made to seem central or peripheral to the rhetorical task at hand and imbue authority. It can realize and enforce interpersonal relationships within the classroom. Action can realize the value of the process of doing science.

We have shown that although less developed than linguistic modes, action is nonetheless a system for meaning-making with conventionalized forms which goes beyond the accepted function of carrying interpersonal relationships. In the social domain of science at any rate, action is a mode.

The analysis action in the science classroom presented in this chapter shows that it is not simply an illustration of writing, rather that action and speech realize different meanings in the multimodal environment of the science classroom and have different *functional specialisms*. Each mode has different meaning potentials and limitations and, perhaps more importantly, their different functional specialisms make different demands on the audience. The shift between modes in the classroom represents a shift in the cognitive and the affective possibilities and demands on the learner. In this way action, gesture, image and speech interweave to convey meaning and to rhetorically shape students' views of the world in complex ways which language alone cannot realize. Teaching and learning are far more than merely linguistic accomplishments.

We suggest that one of the functions of action in the science classroom is to provide the raw materials for the production of texts in terms of results and the students' experiences. The meaning-making process the students are engaged in is a collaborative, material activity deploying scientific equipment according to the generative semiotic codes of the school science classroom. By contrast, the production of texts is an individual activity which deploys the resources of space (e.g. image) and temporality (e.g. writing leaning on speech) using the generic codes which are relevant to the production of texts within the science classroom. In example two the students were involved in transforming the text of the worksheet and the teacher's instructions into actions which they were later required to transform into a written and visual text: the transformative process was text. This transformation between modes has been suggested as the process of realizing meaning (Greimas, 1987; Kress, 2000a). In this way a series of lessons can function to establish a separation between action as meaning (data collection, setting up equipment) and thought as meaning (interpretation and presentation). This leads to a separation of action and self which serves to establish 'doing science' as a systematic, reflexive and objective process.

The investigation can be an event created to represent a 'proper thing'. In short, it may not really be worth taking notice of the results. Nonetheless, the actions are structured as 'going through the motions' so as to make some set of ideas happen. The question for us was: what is the communicative meaning of these actions, what is it that they realized and what is their function? The analysis presented in this chapter suggests that there are two separate things going on in the science lesson which stand in need of separation. First, what science says it is about; and second, what the students say that it is about. The action of the teacher and the students represents hands-on involvement – the construction of props for communication, empirical evidence, measurement and classification as key aspects of 'doing science'. The importance of the direct experience of doing it and seeing it for yourself is emphasized, although not always realized for all students. Students' actions create different experiences of involvement, collaborative working and self-performance, and realize different interpersonal relationships between themselves and teachers. The organization of action in the science classroom, the use of contrast, repetition and the resulting rhythm all serve to realize aspects of the process of 'doing science' and to establish a range of meanings of that process. These meanings are reliant on the interests of students and teachers. For instance, in example two the students' meticulous care and delicacy with regard to some aspects of the investigation and their disregard of other relatively important aspects, as much as their transformation of the purpose of the investigation, realized their different interests within the science classroom.

Focusing on the meaning of action within the science classroom draws attention to important aspects of learning which attention to language alone fails to capture. In particular, the ways in which the experience of being a learner is mediated through interactions between people, objects, equipment and materials is crucial. Drawing attention to how these interactions mediate success or failure focuses attention on the key role of the teacher in establishing and orchestrating successful interactions within the classroom. The analytical approach developed in this chapter draws attention to aspects of action which do not need exhaustive description and analysis but can serve as a model for interpretation, bringing aspects of action in time and place to the teacher's consciousness.

4

Shapes of knowledge

Introduction

The process of writing includes using structures through which we are expected to realize knowledge, for example, various kinds of sentence structures, structures of clauses (relational, transactive), and at larger textual levels, genres. The process of realizing knowledge through these pre-existing social codings is of course never straightforward, nevertheless it is a process which gives knowledge shape. In this chapter we show that the shaping of knowledge occurs in all modes, and that a shift in mode is a shift in these realizational representational means which in turn changes the shape of knowledge – how what is said is 'said'. We show that a shift in mode never amounts merely to saying the same thing in a different mode, rather it involves a deep reshaping of that which is represented.

In this chapter we focus on how the different representational choices made available in the process of reassembling written meanings into the visual (and vice versa) affect shaping of knowledge, reshaping what is said. Of course we realize that implicit in this approach is an assumption which may be highly contentious, namely that knowledge is shapeless unless and until it is realized in some mode, and that there is no knowledge outside of its realization (by which we include of course 'internal' realization/representation). Science is a good test-bed for exploring these ideas because of the specialized forms of representation which are characteristic of it.

In science education information is visually represented in a variety of ways: in different types of graphs, tables, concept maps, food chains, pyramids, etc. Each of these conventions presents information in a distinctive way, includes or excludes specific elements, organizes elements in particular spatial (and by metaphoric extension, conceptual) relationships to each other, and each gives rise to different designs of these elements into textual wholes. In this way, the form of a visual representation foregrounds or suppresses different aspects of information. The form of a representation chosen by teachers and students itself organizes or shapes knowledge in particular ways. As such, form is an integral aspect of the meaning-making process.

In this chapter we analyse two examples of students' text production in the science classroom and show how their teacher's use of visual communication shaped knowledge in order to make it 'convincing'. The first example deals with blood circulation but from the perspective of the students. It discusses the students' production of concept maps and shows how the students used spatial composition and directionality to construct and realize relationships between concepts. The second example deals with energy and focuses on the transformation from a predominantly visual representation to a written representation in a series of three worksheets. It shows how this shift enabled the erasing of difference through the reclassification of the everyday into the scientific.

Our analysis demonstrates:

1 How visually realized shapes of knowledge common to the science classroom produce meaning through conventional spatial arrangements of information which students are expected to be capable of reading and reproducing;

2 How everyday knowledge (low specialized knowledge) in Bernstein's terms (Bernstein, 1996) is transformed into scientific knowledge (highly specialized knowledge);

3 The transformation of meanings in the transition across different modes, and the effects on shapes of knowledge within the science classroom.

Concept maps

Concept maps were developed in science education as a tool to represent changes in students' knowledge structures over time. They are used to emphasize the relationships between and among concepts through the use of the spatial dimension. The arrows between concepts are usually used to indicate a causal or a hierarchical relationship. Our example is taken from the last lesson in a series of five on 'Living Liquid: Blood' with Year 8 students. The teacher introduced the task, gave the students a worksheet containing 20 words as 'concepts', an A3 sheet of white paper, and offered them a model of the process of producing a concept map by showing them how to do so on the whiteboard. His demonstration highlighted the need to link similar ideas through spatial closeness, and by their use of arrows. The teacher suggested taking a central word, blood, and then thinking of what other words linked to it, and explaining the connection. However, the resources for meaning-making within the form of a concept map were not made explicit – how to use spatial relations to create meanings of linking, or how to use arrows or lines to produce particular relationships.

The students were involved in the task of 'disassembling' and 'reassembling' the knowledge they had gained from the four previous lessons (via talk, written text, image and action) in order to make it newly meaningful within the representational constraints and possibilities offered by a concept map. They were engaged with choices and decisions of how to represent this knowledge visually, how to arrange the knowledge spatially, and what connections to make between elements, i.e. the kinds of designs which shape knowledge in new ways and change what is 'said'. However, they had limited knowledge of the resources available to them in this representational task.

The students' concept maps differed greatly from each other, although they were given the same material resources to produce them and had attended the same series of lessons on blood circulation. In particular, their use of the means of composition and directionality as an element in the mode of the visual varied. We argue that the differences between the concept maps are the result of differential understandings of the topic based on differential interest, leading to arrangements of elements to express their specific meanings representing the circulation of the blood in a particular way. Below we present a descriptive analysis of the different ways in which the students used spatial means in composition and directionality to express particular relationships between the concepts, that is, how the students used the meaning resources made available by the form of concept maps to give shape to their knowledge.

Composition: The design of relationships

Kress and van Leeuwen (1996) argue that the composition of images marshals meaningful elements into coherent text in code-specific structures which themselves produce meaning. The structure of the composition provides information about the meaning of the image. A composition may make use of the possibilities of arrangement along the horizontal or vertical axes. Social semiotics argues that for readers of Roman script, the left element in a horizontally arranged composition has the information value of the *given,* the right element has the information value of the *new.* (We might reflect that with the affordances of the computer screen left-to-right might be superseded by the scrolling down of text challenging the deep meaning of left–right by rotating it through 90 degrees.) Conforming to a different principle of western European spatial semiotics, the top element in horizontally polarized compositions has the modal value of the *ideal* (it tends to make an emotive appeal and show us what might be) while the bottom element has the value of the *real,* the empirical, practical showing of 'what is'. The position of represented participants can be either *centred* or *polarized.* An element in the centre of a composition is the nucleus of the information on which all other elements are in some sense dependent. If an element is centred, other participants may be placed to form either a *triptych* or on surrounding *circles.* Alternatively the non-central elements in a centred composition may be in the *margin,* and the centre may be a *mediator* reconciling two polarized elements. As far as the shape of elements is concerned, within western culture circles represent (among other meanings) completeness and cycles of time.

In our analysis of the concept maps produced by the students in this class we draw on the work of Kress and van Leeuwen (1996) to explore how students used composition to express meaningful spatial relationships between the concepts. Centrality, polarization and the use of the page from left to right were among the key compositional design features (representing decisions made in this set of choices by the designers) which informed the students' construction of the concept maps.

Circular compositions

Several of the groups of students used a circular arrangement in their concept maps such as maps A and B (in Figures 4.1 and 4.2 respectively). Where the composition included a circular arrangement of the elements, the thematically focal element was in the centre of the concept map. In each of these instances the word 'Blood' was placed at the centre of the composition and six other words/concepts were arranged immediately around it in a circle.

The students' use of spatial proximity in this way realized specific meanings in relation to blood circulation and accorded different degrees of importance to each of the entities represented. Placing 'blood' in the centre of the composition served to represent it as the most salient element in the concept map and key for understanding and mediating the action shown. The words arranged in a circle immediately around it were given a status deriving from their closeness to the centre. Those entities which were not included in this 'inner circle of involvement' were compositionally distanced from the process of blood circulation. The spatial positioning of these entities realized their lesser importance and further asserted the importance of the central elements.

The students' use of spatial arrangements enabled them to express different understandings of the role of entities in the circulation of the blood. In concept map A (Figure 4.1) the following words/concepts were included in the inner circle arrangement: heart, veins, platelets, red blood cells, white blood cells and plasma. Their inclusion expressed a focus on the movement of the blood (pumped around by the heart) along a particular route (the veins) and the construction of the blood as an 'entity' consisting of different parts (platelets, red

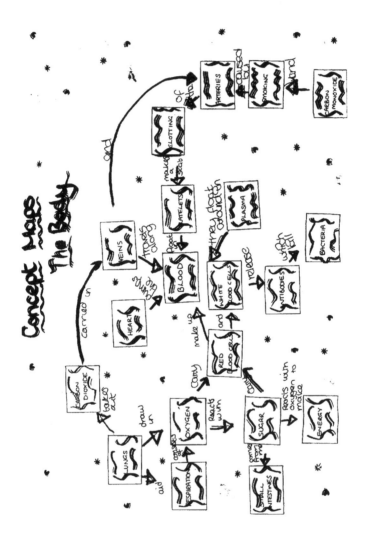

FIGURE 4.1 *Students' concept map A of living liquid.*

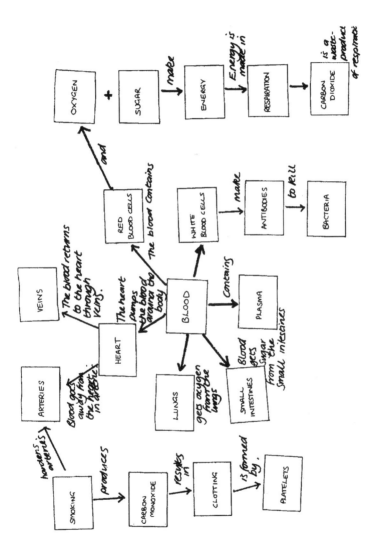

FIGURE 4.2 *Students' concept map B of living liquid.*

blood cells, white blood cells and plasma). Concept map B (Figure 4.2) included different concepts/words in the inner circle: heart, lungs, small intestine, plasma, white blood cells and red blood cells. This spatial arrangement indicated the close involvement in the process of blood circulation of these concepts and again expressed a focus on the movement of the blood and its consisting of different parts but with the addition of the organs (lungs, small intestines) as stopping-off points on the route.

In both concept maps the students' use of spatial arrangements indicated the central role of the entity 'blood', its complexity and the importance of the heart. The notion of movement was present in both concept maps and was shown either as via the veins or in terms of process via the organs. Overall the circular composition of the concept maps encoded blood circulation as a cyclical process with no starting point. In this way the spatial arrangement of the concepts itself made meaning.

Left-to-right arrangement

Concept map C (Figure 4.3) is an example of a left-to-right composition in which the left element has the information value of the *given* and the right element has the information value of the *new*. 'Blood' is placed at the extreme centre-left of the concept map. Two distinct left-to-right narrative-like structures move here from left to right. The far right of the page is occupied by 'energy'. These narrative strands are composed of (i) blood/heart/arteries/veins/platelets/clotting; and (ii) blood/red blood cells/lungs/oxygen/sugar/energy.

Each of the narrative strands focused on one aspect of blood and blood circulation, and reflects the organization of the series of lessons. The first narrative focused on the movement of blood and the processes by which this movement was realized (the production of platelets) and ended (clotting). The second narrative concerned the blood's role in the process of getting and converting entities (oxygen and sugar) into energy. These two compositional arrangements show the blood operating at different levels to realize different functions.

Nonetheless their outcome is the same: energy. Placing blood at the centre-left gave it the value of the starting point – the given. Placing the starting point mid-way on the vertical axis between 'real'

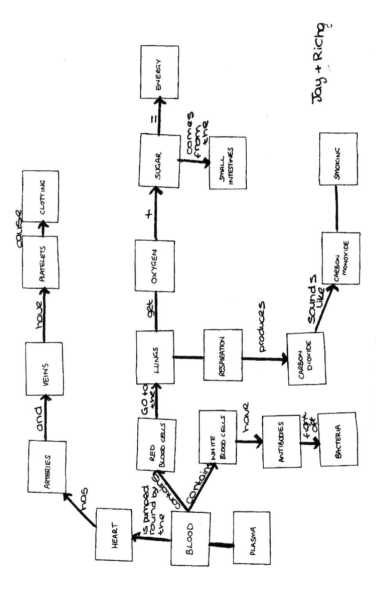

FIGURE 4.3 Students' concept map C of living liquid

and 'ideal' perhaps suggests that this student did not wish to make a commitment in this dimension.

In contrast to representations of the circulation of the blood as a cycle, the use of a linear left-to-right compositional arrangement implied that there was a starting point to blood circulation. In this case horizontal distance was used as an indicator of time and process. Spatial distance from the starting point became the measure of distance of involvement in the process of blood circulation. Whereas blood was represented spatially as a starting point (on the left), energy was represented as the visual outcome – the new. Through the use of left-to-right arrangements, the narrative was one of a conceptual transformation from blood to energy.

Triptych

Several of the concept maps, for example, A and B (Figures 4.1 and 4.2), used a triptych composition: a panel on the left of the page, a central panel, and a panel on the right of the page. Triptych compositional structures combine both left-to-right arrangements and centrality. As already stated, an entity in a central compositional position has the value of mediating the action on both the left-hand side of the concept map (the given) and the right (the new). The concept maps with a triptych arrangement represented blood circulation as a centrally organized cycle, but the arrangement of the concepts/words across the left and right panels of the composition varied. Tables 4.1 and 4.2

Table 4.1 Triptych in concept map A (Figure 4.1)

Left	Middle	Right
carbon dioxide	blood cycle	clotting
lungs		arteries
respiration		smoking
oxygen		carbon monoxide
small intestine		
sugar		
energy		

Table 4.2 Triptych in concept map B (Figure 4.2)

Left	Middle	Right
smoking	blood cycle	oxygen
carbon monoxide		sugar
clotting		energy
platelets		carbon dioxide

highlight how the two groups' arrangement of the concepts/words within a triptych compositional structure realized different meanings.

The compositional arrangement of words in concept map A (shown in Table 4.1) included the elements involved in respiration and digestion to the left of the concept map, and the elements associated with disease to the right. In this case the blood cycle in the centre of the composition was presented as mediating between the healthy natural process of respiration and the potential for illness (in the form of smoking and, more abstractly, clotting).

Concept map B (Figure 4.2) used the same triptych arrangement and the same semiotic resources but told a different story. The blood cycle remained in the centre of the composition but the arrangement of words/concepts on the left and the right altered its meaning. The potential for bad health, in the form of smoking, carbon monoxide and clotting, was arranged on the left of the concept map, realizing the value of given. Respiration, the process of producing energy and the expulsion of waste products (carbon dioxide) were represented on the right. This arrangement of the concepts served to realize the mediating role of blood as cleansing the bad (smoking, carbon monoxide and clotting) in order to produce the new (oxygen, sugar, energy, respiration), and to expel waste (carbon dioxide).

The students each used triptych compositional arrangements differently. We argue that their uses realized their different understandings and interests in relation to the functions of the circulation of the blood: the first to balance, the second to restore and cleanse. Perhaps these different constructions of the blood can be read as the students' visual-spatial expressions of their different understandings of risk.

Top-to-bottom arrangement

In several of the students' concept maps the concepts/words were arranged top-to-bottom on the page. The concept map in Figure 4.3 combined left-to-right with top-to-bottom arrangements to make meaning.

The elements in the three sections of Figure 4.3 (top, middle, bottom) form different narratives as shown in Table 4.3. At the top, a narrative on the movement of the blood; in the middle, a narrative on the process production of energy; and at the bottom, a narrative of disease and ill health. The arrangement at the top of the page represented an ideal of the blood as an internal event, the arrangement at the bottom of the page represented the function of blood as mediating disease from the external (smoking and bacteria).

The spatial arrangement of these three narratives from top to bottom itself created a narrative: the blood moved around the veins and then went to the organs and produced energy which mediated the body's ability to respond to disease. This can also be read as the top (ideal) as knowledge, the middle (mediator) as knowledge converted to actual process, and the bottom (real) as the consequences of that process.

The students who made the concept map D in Figure 4.4 used a top-to-bottom spatial arrangement to different effect. The map is divided into a top, middle and bottom through the arrangement of the concepts/words and consists of one partially cyclical

Table 4.3 Top-to-bottom arrangement in concept map C (Figure 4.3)

Top (ideal)	heart/arteries/veins/platelets/clotting
Middle (mediator)	red blood cells/lungs/oxygen/sugar/energy/ small intestines
Bottom (real)	plasma/white blood cells/respiration/antibodies/ carbon dioxide/bacteria/carbon monoxide/ smoking

Table 4.4 Top-to-bottom arrangement in concept map D (Figure 4.4)

Top (ideal)	veins/arteries/plasma/heart/blood/white blood cells/antibodies/bacteria/red blood cells/platelets/clotting
Middle (mediator)	lungs
Bottom (real)	carbon monoxide/oxygen/sugar/small intestines/smoking/carbon dioxide/energy/respiration

arrangement at the top of the page and another at the bottom, between which sits 'lungs'. These partial cycles attended to different bodily processes highlighted by the series of lessons. The arrangement at the top focused on the circulation of the blood, the one at the bottom on the digestive process and respiration, as shown in Table 4.4.

The concept map represented the circulation of the blood as two cycles or routes. The entities in the top half of the page represented the movement of the blood from the heart through the arteries; the cycle in the bottom half of the page represented respiration and digestion. The top-bottom arrangement spatially represented the body as involved in discrete processes: blood circulation, digestion and respiration. Blood circulation was represented as a distinct process separate from digestion and respiration. It was not presented as a key part of either of these processes. The positioning of the lungs between the top and the bottom cycles represented them as the central concept connecting the two cycles, perhaps representing breathing as the (most important) mediating signifier of life, rather than blood. This compositional design reflected the teacher's presentation of the circulation of the blood initially as a single loop and later as a complex double loop (as described in Chapter 2) which in turn reflects the history of the understanding of blood circulation. In this way the concept map represents both the simplicity of the blood as an (historically) ideal vision, and the complexity of its route as a reality.

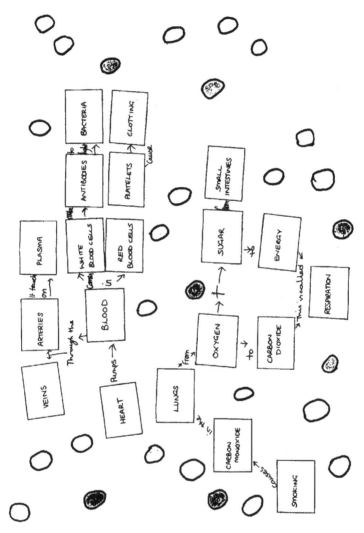

FIGURE 4.4 *Students' concept map D of living liquid.*

The use of arrows to construct conceptual relations

In addition to spatial arrangements the students used arrows and lines to visually indicate relationships between concepts. Arrows are a semiotic resource which can be used to express a range of meanings. They vary in thickness, vectoriality, length, boldness (indicating modality) and in being solid or dotted.

Directionality

The students used directionality to realize meaning. In concept maps A and B, in which the students represented blood as the central entity (Figures 4.1 and 4.2), we can see that the directionality of the arrows differs (Figure 4.5).

In map A the arrows point out from the blood to the surrounding entities; in B blood remains the central entity but the arrows point to it from the surrounding entities. In A the central concept of 'blood' is expanded in order to understand the other entities. In B the importance of the other entities is asserted because even though 'blood' is compositionally signalled as a central entity, it is constructed by the action of the other entities. The students are using the semiotics of arrows in different ways, struggling with a new and unarticulated mode to realize meanings.

Transactional processes

The students used horizontal arrows to indicate transactional processes (for example pumps, returns, produces, fight off, releases) which visually identified the actor and the goal in the process. Examples are given below at Figure 4.6.

In some instances the students showed these processes by using horizontal lines to connect the words, in other cases they used vertical lines (Figure 4.6b), and in yet others they used diagonal lines (Figure 4.6a). They combined directionality and vectoriality to establish relationships between the concepts. The combination of direction and a strong diagonal vector served to visually intensify the

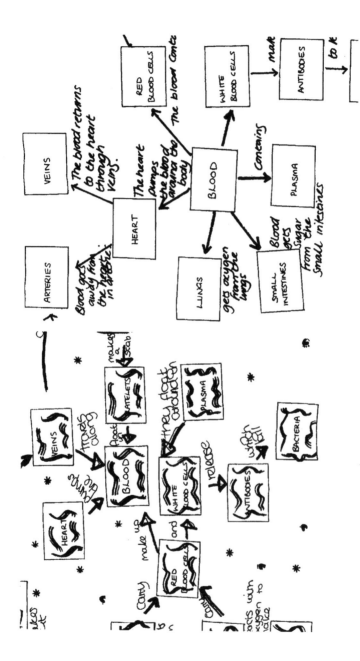

FIGURE 4.5 *Comparison of directionality of arrows in concept maps A and B.*

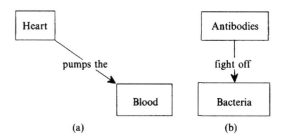

FIGURE 4.6 *Transactional processes.*

force of the action being represented. In this way both blood and the heart were represented as powerful actors within the concept maps. In contrast, the bacteria and clotting were consistently represented as the goal of a transitive action (they were always acted on, never the actor) and represented as entities outside of the process of blood circulation: a goal of the blood circulation, not as actors in it.

Relational processes

The elements selected as nodes (boxes, etc.) in the maps are mainly object-like (blood, lungs, heart). Arrows linking them are often processes (e.g. pumps, travels along) but are sometimes logical/ spatial links (e.g. contains). Other lexical links often used in concept maps, but not used by these students at all, are 'is a case of', 'has a property', 'has as example' and so on, but these are used in the left-to-right narrative structure of Figure 4.3, in which the layout expresses narrative elements. However, here the narrative is linked by logical steps – classificational or relational processes such as have, get, comes from, need, sounds like).

Students used lines and arrows to indicate relational processes (connections) between entities, for example consists of, make up, or is formed by. In some cases the students used vertical or horizontal lines to link these elements (Figure 4.7a), in others they used hierarchical relational trees (e.g. Figures 4.7b and c below).

In this way the students used spatial arrangements and arrows to indicate whole-part relations. In Figure 4.7b the students used spatial arrangement and arrows to separate the negative

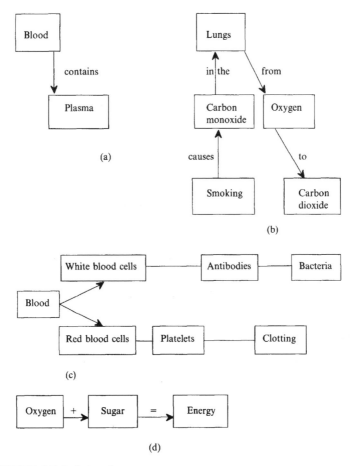

FIGURE 4.7 *Relational processes.*

unnatural processes associated with the lungs (carbon monoxide and smoking) from the positive 'natural' aspects (oxygen, carbon dioxide and respiration). In Figure 4.7c students used the same resources to indicate the different parts and functions of the blood: white blood cells produce antibodies and 'kill' bacteria; red blood cells produce platelets which clot. In other instances (e.g. Figure 4.7d) the students used spatial arrangements and arrows to show the relationship A = B, or to name processes between them.

Visual and written narratives

The students integrated visual and linguistic resources into their concept maps to different degrees. Some relied on the visual to make meaning and used the concept boxes and arrows to represent the players in the process (e.g. Figure 4.8a).

Others integrated the visual and the linguistic, and used the concept boxes to visually stand for themselves in a written sentence (e.g. Figure 4.8b). Some students used the visual and the linguistic separately. Each was used to articulate discrete meanings visually and linguistically. In this case the students wrote out the whole sentence alongside the visual display (e.g. Figure 4.8c). A few of the maps drew on genre conventions other than the linguistic narrative. These students used the mathematical convention of the equation to assert the relationships between concepts in their maps in the mathematical form of a sentence (e.g. Figure 4.8d).

The students used visual and written elements in their concept maps to give shape to their understanding of blood circulation. Here we show how the students used the visual and the written resources available to them to realize specific relationships between the concepts. In particular we focus on the central design of concept map B (Figure 4.2) to show that the students' use of these two semiotic

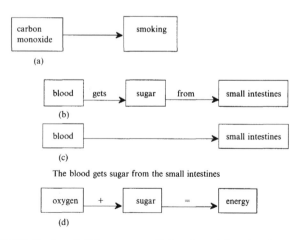

FIGURE 4.8 *Students' different uses of visual-spatial and written modes.*

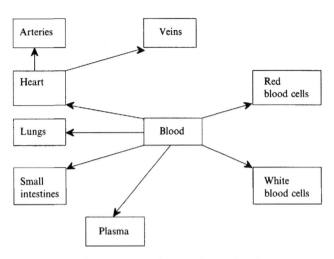

FIGURE 4.9 *Visual narrative of central panel of concept map B (Figure 4.2).*

modes created distinct 'recounts' and therefore distinct meanings about blood circulation. The concept maps can be viewed almost as two layers of meaning: a visual layer (Figure 4.9) and a written layer (Figure 4.10). These interact to realize meanings: sometimes the meaning of the visual contradicted the meaning of the written and vice versa, sometimes they reinforced one another.

A comparison of the visual and the written recounts in the central design of the concept map shows that they differ in terms of the direction with which they endow processes and the actors and goals in the process. The six arrows coming out from the central word/concept 'blood' serve to visually represent its central role in the processes displayed. 'Blood' defines the other words/concepts and is represented as the actor in a series of unidirectional transactive actions on the heart, the red blood cells, the veins, the arteries, the lungs, the small intestines, plasma, and white blood cells. Through the use of arrows the heart was visually represented as a secondary actor. In contrast it is the heart which is shown as pumping the blood in the written element of the concept map. Linguistically the heart is presented as the actor, the blood as its goal. In the writing 'blood' is shown as 'returning to the heart through the veins' whereas visually the direction is reversed, as the heart

Blood goes away from the heart in arteries.
The blood returns to the heart through veins.
The blood contains [red blood cells].
The heart pumps the blood around the body.
[Blood] gets oxygen from the lungs.
Blood gets sugar from the small intestine.
[Blood] contains [plasma].
[Blood] ————————>[white blood cells].

FIGURE 4.10 *Written recounts of central design of concept map B (Figure 4.2).*

acts on the veins. The visual and the written elements provide different accounts, different ways of conferring importance, different roles for the 'players', and different versions of meaning. This suggests to us that (i) perhaps the students were struggling with the new meaning-making resources made available to them in the visual mode via the genre of 'concept map' to make coherent meanings; and (ii) the visual and written elements attended to different aspects of the meaning.

It is clear that there are not many stable or fixed conventions for how nodes and links should be used or arranged in concept maps, nor for how text elements should be used in relation to visual elements and arrangements. For this very reason, they are a very 'open' semiotic resource; they readily display different choices made about what to represent and how to represent it. These choices do, as we expected, provide evidence of differences in interest, and of creative and individual use of the representational resources on offer.

Some of the main structures chosen are:

1. Spatial arrangements to carry relational meaning, including hierarchy and importance, in which case:
   - nodes realize object-like representation;
   - links realize narrative (process) meanings.

2. Spatial arrangements represent narrative and sequence, in which case:
   - nodes as before realize 'objects';
   - links realize relational meaning.

Summary

Three distinct points are implicit from our analysis. First, even though these young people have not been given explicit instructions in the grammar of visual design, they are actively experimenting with it and are in fact well on the way to fashioning one for themselves. Even our relatively light analysis shows aspects of that grammar, and it would not be difficult to describe it in somewhat more systematic terms. Just as young people make their way into the grammars of speech and of writing, so these young people are making their way into the grammar of the visual, in this as in other genres.

Second, as we have just pointed out, in one sense the fact that there is no grammar leaves this resource more 'open', less constrained than in resources where grammar is pronounced. This allows the ready expression of the 'interests' of the young meaning-makers, in the ways we have shown. From a pedagogic point of view the first question here is not 'Did they get this right or not?' but rather 'What is the interest that they are expressing here, which underlies and motivates this specific representation of the issue at hand?' If the teacher's interest is in learning, then this is excellent evidence both of what was learned and of the motivations for the learning that took place. Third, in time the need to have reliable means for assessing visual representations made in school will become pressing, and this approach promises one route to the development of such means. Unless we know how to read these texts as full evidence of learning, there is no point in even contemplating forms of assessment.

From picture cards to written facts: Rubbing out difference

Our second example is drawn from the first lesson in a series of six on the topic 'Energy' with Year 9 students. The lesson focused on constructing 'energy' as a quantifiable entity. Through its potential to be quantified, the often intangible entity energy was brought into existence and made concrete. The lesson rested on the use of three worksheets. The first worksheet introduced by the teacher (see Figure 4.11) required the students to pair picture cards of energy sources and jobs done with energy. The second worksheet (see Figure 4.12) provided a table-like structure in which students ranked types of energy according to the amount of energy each provided. The third worksheet (see Figure 4.13) consisted of a series of incomplete sentence structures into which students entered the names of the missing energy value.

As a quick look at the three worksheets reveals, each organized information in different ways: the first visually, the second in tabular form and the third in narrative-like sentences. Each worksheet drew on different representational means to realize meaning. In the following section, we discuss how each worksheet shaped the students' knowledge of energy as an entity in specific ways and how the worksheets worked as a series to reshape everyday knowledge into scientific knowledge.

Worksheet 1

Worksheet 1 was predominantly visual. It classified the entities in terms of source and use (cause and effect), it quantified them in terms of size, and related the pairs in terms of best fit (an estimate). The students worked in pairs or small groups. Each group of students laid all their picture cards on the table. Some students sorted the cards into two groups – source and use – and then into pairs of source and use; others sorted them directly into pairs of source and use; others initially attempted to sort the cards alphabetically (according to the letters on each card).

Some of the members of the source category were usual in terms of everyday ideas of energy as natural things that burn (e.g. tree, paraffin, coal, meths, petrol), others were more clearly socially formed objects (e.g. pencil, chair) and were less often immediately classified by the students as a source of energy. However, the framing of the image on each of the picture cards offered the students a visual clue in classifying them. The pictures of sources were framed by a rectangle with sharp 90-degree corners, while the pictures of uses were framed with a rectangle with rounded corners.

The classification of entities as either sources or uses established the members of each category as the same: paraffin became like

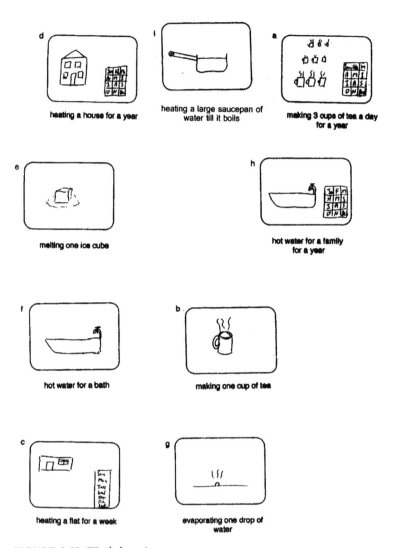

FIGURE 4.11 *Worksheet 1 on energy.*

a candle, a chair became like a pencil. The picture cards visually represented the members of each category as being the same size (some used a representation of the calendar year as an index of amount). The students had to use their everyday knowledge in order to rank the members of each category in terms of size. Once all

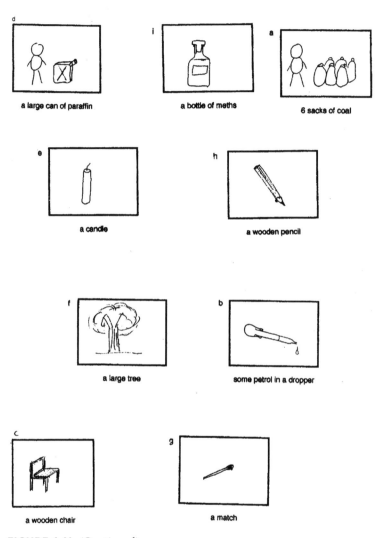

a large can of paraffin

a bottle of meths

6 sacks of coal

a candle

a wooden pencil

a large tree

some petrol in a dropper

a wooden chair

a match

FIGURE 4.11 *(Continued)*

members of the categories had been ranked in this way, the source–use pairs could be established. This classification process provided the students with a structure which enabled them to see these entities differently than in the everyday: a chair temporarily became a source of energy instead of a piece of furniture or something on which to sit still. This process reshaped the students relationships to the entities and in so doing constructed the entity 'energy' as beyond the realm of the students' everyday experiences – taking up unexpected shapes, existing anywhere and so on.

The cards afforded a flexible process whereby the students moved them into new configurations which expressed and realized their changing views, eliminated potential pairs and reordered the cards. When the final source-use pairs were recorded by the students in their exercise books the process of achieving the pairs was lost. The shift from picture cards to written statements solidified their decisions, removed any ambiguity expressed during the task and produced stable facts.

The worksheet utilized students' existing knowledge of energy and size from the realm of the everyday (energy as 'fuel' as contrasted with worksheet 2 in which energy is 'food', 'sun', 'moving things') in order to build a new classification of energy by 'amounts of use'. This provided the basis for the students' acceptance of worksheet 2, which was built on the notion of energy as a quantifiable entity existing in a range of forms. The notion of sources of energy as entities which have to undergo a process was implicit in the first worksheet (e.g. trees, candles, paraffin, meths and coal all have to burn) which prepared the students to know how to read the food categories in worksheet 2 (the biscuit has to be eaten).

Worksheet 2

Worksheet 2 used linguistic representations of the entities; however, the visual representation of relations between the entities was paramount in the composition of the page. The elements were classified in terms of energy value explicitly measured in kilojoules. Here the structure of the table related the entities to one another through comparison. The students ranked the entities given within each of four categories (food, moving things, using electricity and the sun) into the columns of the table in terms of the estimated size of 'energy value'. This task drew on students' everyday knowledge of events. Once entered into the table this information could be read along the table rows in order to compare energy values across

	Food	Moving things	Using electricity	The Sun
10 000 kJ				
1000 kJ				
100 kJ				
10 kJ				

a a biscuit	a a car travels down a short road	a using an electric fire for 3 hours	a sunlight on a person for 20 seconds
b a loaf of bread	b walking 5 miles	b using a light bulb for half an hour	b sunlight on a small plant for 20 minutes
c a spoon of milk	c walking to the top of a 6 storey building	c using a TV for 5 hours	c sunlight on a house for 2 minutes
d a packet of crisps	d a car travels 10 miles	d using an electric fire for 10 seconds	d sunlight on a person for half an hour

FIGURE 4.12 *Worksheet 2 on energy.*

the categories. The activity of ordering demanded by the structure of the table gave the students access to the scientific knowledge of the energy value of each entity – it transformed the students' knowledge of the everyday (low specialized knowledge) into scientific knowledge (highly socialized knowledge). In this way the table both highlighted and suppressed features of the entities to make them appear similar, or different. For example, the low specialized knowledge of the difference(s) between a loaf of bread and a car travelling ten miles (e.g. taste, cost or the entity consuming the energy) was 'rubbed out', and instead constructed as a similarity in terms of the highly specialized knowledge of energy value in kilojoules.

Worksheet 3

Visual communication had less significance for meaning here than in the other worksheets. Worksheet 3 is predominantly a written text consisting of sentences to be completed. Each sentence classified two entities as the same in terms of their energy values: 'The energy value of [entity A] is the same as [entity B]'. Each sentence presented an entity from one everyday category (e.g. food) as being equal to an entity from a different everyday category (e.g. the sun). In this way, worksheet 3 offered the students a narrative-like structure with which to newly interpret the information they had entered into the

---

Comparing energy values

You will need to use the sheet 'More energy values' and the other sheet 'Using fuels to heat things'.

You need to pick the things which have the same energy value, for example:

The energy value of a biscuit is the same as that of sunlight shining on a small plant for 2 minutes (100 kJ).

Now do the following – copy the sentence, filling in the end:

1. The energy to make a car move 10 miles is the same as ... (use the column 'Energy transferred to heat things').
2. The energy value of a loaf of bread is the same as ... (use the column 'The Sun').
3. The energy value of a candle is the same as ... ('Energy transferred to thing being heated').
4. The energy transferred to make one cup of tea is the same as ... ('Moving things').
5. The energy used by an electric fire in 3 hours is the same as ... ('Energy transferred from fuel').
6. The energy value of a bottle of meths is the same as ... ('Using electricity').
7. The energy of sunlight shining on a person for 20 seconds is the same as ... ('Moving things').
8. The energy transferred to make the hot water for a bath is the same as ... ('Food').
9. The energy used by a TV in 5 hours is the same as ... ('The Sun').
10. The energy to walk to the top of a 5 storey building is the same as ... ('Energy transferred from fuel').

Did any of these surprise you? If so, explain why.

Try making up some more of your own.

FIGURE 4.13 *Worksheet 3 on energy.*

table on worksheet 2. Rather than requiring the students to read the information in the table on worksheet 2 in the form that they had thought of and entered it (as the ranking of the energy values of members within four discrete groups), the sentence structures in worksheet 3 required the students to read the information in the table in worksheet 2 across its rows so as to think of the entities in each row as members of a discrete group of 'energy values'. The structure of worksheet 3 demanded that the students draw out the table's transformation of their everyday knowledge into a scientific expression of knowledge as 'energy value'. The final worksheet in the series completed the transformation from everyday knowledge to scientific knowledge.

The sequential shaping of knowledge

The students' interactions with the worksheets involved them in the process of the gradual construction of the entity 'energy'. Each worksheet shaped the students' knowledge of energy in a specific way through the use of a foregrounded mode which brought into focus *classification, relations between entities* and *quantification*. The central differences in the conceptual work required by the three worksheets are summarized in Table 4.5.

Table 4.5 Summary of the central differences in the conceptual work required by the three worksheets on energy

	Worksheet 1	Worksheet 2	Worksheet 3
Conceptual work	predominantly visual	linguistic and visual	predominantly linguistic
Classification	source–use (cause and effect)	energy value in kilojoules	energy values
Quantification	size	kilojoules	sameness
Relations between elements	match best fit	comparison	substitution

The worksheets shifted from the predominantly visual (worksheet 1) to linguistic with visual as a means of organization (worksheet 2) to predominantly linguistic text (worksheet 3). As discussed elsewhere (see Chapters 2, 4 and 5), visual and linguistic modes of communication each have particular constraints and limitations, and each is able to do some things better than the others. In this way the shift in mode of communication is a part of the shaping of knowledge. The first worksheet establishes a connection between source and use. The second quantifies the relationship between sources and use. The third provides a canonical expression of the relationship in an equation of source and use. The progression from worksheet 1 to 3 involves an increase in the constraints on the agency of the students and their 'ownership' of the tasks.

Measurement

In the first worksheet the predominance of the visual mode encoded measurement as 'physical size' (in some cases combined with duration over time). Energy was portrayed as quantifiable by drawing on students' everyday understanding of size as a measure of quantity. The worksheet task required students to give a rough estimate of 'amount of energy needed'. The second worksheet again drew on students' knowledge of the everyday to measure energy, however, it required students to place this into the metric scale of the kilojoule. The inaccuracy of these measurements was implicit in the lack of delicacy between the values (i.e. 10,000, 1000, 100 and 10). Worksheet 3 required students to put the information into a standardized verbal form. The estimates of the previous worksheets were replaced by the factual statement '. . . is the same as . . .' (rather than 'is similar to'). In this way the final worksheet reshaped the students' everyday knowledge expressed initially as a rough visual estimate into scientific knowledge expressed as an objective written fact.

Stability

The picture cards required the students to classify the categories of source and use. The nature of the task was relatively open, enabling the students to resort the cards, change their minds and express ambiguities. The final pairs were recorded without the need to be explicit about the relationship between the source and use beyond their fitting together. Any ambiguities expressed during the process of matching source and use were left quietly, unrecorded. In the second worksheet specific features of the entities were abstracted – their energy value in joules became the yardstick by which the questions of the lesson were answered. The third worksheet translated this information into verbal relational form as canonical, but away from the objective quantification of value. The factual statements gave a stable shape to the relationships between entities.

Agency

The role of the students' agency became more constrained as the lesson progressed. The constraints on their thinking presented by the structure of the worksheets increased with the shift from visual to written communication, and the shift from everyday 'low specialized' knowledge to scientific 'highly specialized' knowledge. In worksheet 1 the students compared sources and jobs done, they shifted the picture cards around, reasoned, changed their minds, rearranged and reclassified the cards until they reached a best fit. In worksheet 2 the processes of classification and comparison were camouflaged in the layout of the table so that the table, rather than the students, made the comparisons.

In this case, bringing the everyday into the table led to the revelation of the unusual and the scientific (e.g. in energy terms 'bread is the same as petrol'). The students' everyday knowledge ('a loaf of bread is bigger than a biscuit') was transformed by placing it within a scientific frame. Once the information was placed in the columns, the table made available the energy values across the rows. Thus the structure of the table transformed the everyday ranking of entities into energy values (kilojoules). In worksheet 3 the students had to read off the table in worksheet 2 to complete the sentences. They had no freedom of agency (the worksheet even instructed them which column to read the data from). The students' everyday knowledge had been trapped into the format of the worksheets and shaped beyond recognition to become scientific truth. With this decrease in students' agency came the increase in 'factuality'.

Finally, the worksheets can be seen as steps to the students' imagining or 'rubbing away' the differences between entities of the everyday so that they could be conceived of as scientifically identical. These steps were necessary to enable students to see the essence of the entity 'energy' beyond their everyday experience of it. What is at work here is the ability to conceive of different objects as the same and to be able to quantify them as amounts of the same substance. The activity invited by the general format of worksheets serves to camouflage the tightly structured nature of the task in which the students are involved in practising 'saying it like it is'.

A central issue in learning and teaching abstractions such as 'energy' (or 'force', etc.) is seeing different particular things as similar. For example, first seeing burning wood in a fire as 'like' burning petrol in an engine and then seeing both as 'like' digesting ('burning') food.

Visual representations are good at being particular (the visual is not good at showing 'burning' because it always has to show 'burning *this*'), but the actions of arranging and sorting visual elements is a process of abstraction through comparison. So it is reasonable to begin with *abstracting action on particulars*. Abstraction is first dealt with as (physical) *action*, and only later as objectified and verbal.

Conclusion

It is clear that the visual and other representations are more than merely pedagogic devices, though it is likely that this is how the teachers and students envisage them. They enable scientific meanings to be constructed and shifts of kinds of meanings to take place which are more than mere progression in easy steps. Rather, they enable students to express ideas and make meanings which neither they nor the teacher could readily do in a different mode of communication or in one mode alone.

5

Rethinking learning in the multimodal environment: Learning to be scientific

Introduction

The multimodal environment of the science classroom described in the previous chapters has profound implications for thinking about learning. Central among these is the relationship between mode and 'thinking'. If, as we have argued earlier, the affordances of different modes enable different representational work to be done so that information and meanings are shaped and conveyed in distinctly different ways, then it follows that each mode entails different cognitive work and has different conceptual and cognitive consequences. So in this and the following two chapters we focus on two connected issues: what it means to learn within the multimodal environment of the science classroom, and what learning is and how it might need to be rethought in the context of a theory of multimodality.

We approach students' texts (and the decisions students engaged with in producing them) as providing the best way into understanding these two issues. Students' texts are an expression of how they engaged with knowledge in the classroom and represent the best form of evidence of learning. We explore how students use the resources made available to them by the teacher in the classroom and from other sources (e.g. other lessons, the television, their experiences and interests outside of school, etc.) to construct meanings and to produce their representations, which realize their versions of entities and concepts and show how they see themselves as 'learners of science'. In our approach learning is a transformative action of sign-making (through selection, altering the focus, adaptation and the introduction of new elements) in which students are involved in the active remaking of the signs which have been available to them as resources motivated by the context of the lesson and by their own interests, which may factor in their sense of the teacher's interest but will never be identical with it.

Learning as a process of sign-making

Our understanding of the process of learning as *a dynamic process of sign-making* is informed by social semiotics (Hodge and Kress, 1988). We view the ensemble of the situated communicative actions of the teacher as semiotic material which contributes importantly to the resources involved in students' production of texts in the science classroom, though we can see in the data we have that students constantly draw on all kinds of other resources from all kinds of other contexts of their interest. In this way, we treat the students' texts as semiotic objects, *signs* which mediate their responses to the communicative actions of the classroom and which are expressive of their interests in that environment. Thus they offer one kind of evidence of what their thinking may have been like.

We see meaning-making as a motivated activity in which the interests of the sign-maker (in this case the teacher and the students) is expressed through his or her selection of apt and plausible signifiers for the expression of their meaning in a given context, in an always new sign (Kress, 1997). This means (profoundly from the point of view of learning) that signs are never repetitions, reproductions or copies of the teacher's sign. The students' signs are always transformations of the resources that were available to them, made in the light of their interest at the point of making the sign. Learning is thus always transformative, innovative and creative.

We are interested in how students transform the materials (both the structural and the content aspects of the teacher's communication) through the selection, adaptation of elements presented, and introduction of new elements. We are interested in how students use the resources made available to them in the classroom, from the teacher as much as from other sources, to construct meaning. Seen from a different perspective, this is the process of learning. Rather than trying to get at the cognitive process of students' learning directly (even if such a thing were possible), we focus on the outcome of this process in the form of signs made, whether as whole texts or parts of texts, though always on the full multimodal ensemble. We take these signs to be evidence of the cognitive processes the students have engaged in. As we have said, these signs are also the result of the teacher's previous actions, again transformed by the students.

Students' texts can thus be analysed as traces of the choices made by them from the resources which were available to them, which they saw as pertinent at the moment of choice, in conformity with their interest *vis-à-vis* the topic. The transformations which link their text to the text that constitutes the original resources are then the evidence of the work they engaged in, constantly guided by their interest. In that work the initial resource set has become transformed, but so has the internal 'state' of those who have been the transformers – they are not who they were before – and it is here that 'learning' resides. In saying that a series of transformations links the texts/signs produced by students to the texts that constituted the available source texts we are not in any way claiming that we or anyone else could hope to identify and specify them. Such a claim remains a hypothesis. But in many cases, some documented in this book, we can see the traces of the source texts whether from the teacher's speech, the textbooks or worksheets, the students' own talk, or at times from recoverable sources from outside the school, such as popular media texts for instance.

At any rate, the multimodal approach demands the most serious reading of the signs made by students to see the consequences, possibilities and limitations of their representational choices in terms of mode, elements and arrangements. An easy dismissal of a student text becomes impossible because for the teacher even the text which shows ostensibly a refusal by the student to engage with the resources can with this reading reveal the principles of the lack of engagement – a valuable pedagogic resource for the teacher.

A social theory of communication enables us to view language and literacy practices as resources for making social meanings in the world. Extending our view of communication beyond speech and writing to include other modes of meaning-making (e.g. gesture, visual communication) highlights the need to consider the ways in which these modes express social meanings. In this way, a multimodal social semiotic approach to students' texts opens the way to seeing differences between students' texts not as markers of their individual aesthetic (whether expressed through visual or other material and sensory means) but as a serious expression of different interests; as a transformation into new signs of those of the teacher made in a wide range of modes and materials.

Approaching learning as part of a dynamic, complex process of sign-making in which teachers shape ideas realized in a multiplicity of modes and genres to be learned through a plurality of communicative means so as to make these ideas convincing to students, re-opens the question of why students' texts vary. Nowadays, viewing the learning process as the transmission of knowledge from teacher to student is not the dominant approach in the West (though there are signs of a return to this situation). Despite this, the response to differences between students' texts still tends to be viewed as an indication of students' failure to correctly read (or reproduce) the stable messages encoded in a teacher's communications. The multimodal approach insists that variation between students' texts is an expression of students' differing interests. That is, all students' texts can be read as their shaping of meaning in the most apt and plausible way with the resources available to them in a specific context. For example, aspects of the materiality of a text can reveal traces of the cognitive work involved in producing it: and can be seen as one form of evidence of learning.

The physical characteristics of students' texts in the classroom have rarely been attended to in educational research. Where attention has been given it has provided a link between the study of texts and the study of practices, giving insight into children's literacy practices (Ormerod and Ivanic, 1999). The visual and linguistic resources students draw on to make meaning in the science classroom can be viewed as the cultural working of a medium. The medium is worked and shaped over time into regular forms of representations (e.g. a grammar) and becomes the material (signifier) for the stuff of naming (sign). In this way these forms of representation reflect the material, cultural-historical functional specialization of visual and linguistic modes of communication, that is, the material potentials of visual and linguistic resources have been developed over time in ways which enable the realization of particular meanings. Students are engaged in many complex decisions when selecting how to materially represent something. For them, as for all sign-makers, form and meaning are interconnected and motivated: form is meaning.

In this chapter and the following two we explore through detailed analysis of students' texts the ways in which students in the science classroom conceptualize entities and topics, transforming elements of the teacher's rhetorical account. We focus on this as one form of evidence of learning.

The first example, dealt with in this chapter, focuses on students' texts (visual and written) produced during a lesson on onion cells. We analyse how Year 7 students made sense of and transformed the teacher's requirements to produce a 'scientific text'. Through detailed social semiotic analysis we characterize the way the students engaged with the task of 'being scientific' and how 'scientificness' emerged differently in the texts of four students. We draw attention to the different functions of the visual and the written elements of the students' texts and how these realized 'scientificness'. Through our analysis we demonstrate the pedagogic potential of a multimodal approach to classroom interaction and text analysis.

Pupils' signs as evidence of learning: Emergent expressions of scientificness

In this chapter we exemplify our theoretical approach to learning in order to characterize, from the students' perspective, how the rhetorics of the science classroom are related to learning. The two students who produced texts (Figures 5.1 and 5.2) participated in the same lesson and had the same materials to work with yet, as a quick look at the texts shows, they produced distinctly different texts. It has been suggested that these differences are simply the result of individual readings of the events in the lesson, a consequence of the students' lack of attention, or their poor writing and drawing skills. We suggest that they can be better explained by seeing them as the expression of the different stances each student adopted to the recording of their experience of learning, their response to the protocol of 'being scientific', and their realization of this visually and linguistically, and the students' engagement with the recontextualized genres of schooled knowledges available to them in the task. We highlight the students' use of visual and linguistic resources to realize distinct meanings, thereby emphasizing the importance for a science teacher of attending to the visual elements of the texts produced by students in the classroom and within educational research more generally.

Reading multimodal texts in the science classroom

The texts which we analyse here come from a lesson centred on looking at the cells of an onion under the microscope. They are the students' recordings of what they saw and what they did. The materials on which the students could draw were the teacher's talk (in particular his use of two analogies for cells: a brick and a honeycomb), his instructions, worksheets, the materials and equipment for the experiment, and the students' talk with one another as they engaged with the task. The teacher offered the students worksheets to help them in their task and which also served as models of a 'scientific text'. The teacher gave direct verbal instructions concerning three areas of making the text: composition and labelling, standard ways of drawing in science, and ways of reporting an experiment. He asked the students to divide the page in their exercise books horizontally into two halves and to draw the image of the onion cells in the bottom half of the page and later to write 'What I did' in the top half of the page. The relationship of the image to the writing as set out in the teacher's instructions suggests that he intended the image to be read as the actualization of the writing, the result of the experiment.

The switch in mode from image to writing served further to mark a clear boundary between the events of 'seeing' and 'doing', i.e. the compositional structure of the text to be produced encoded process and result as two discrete categories using two distinct modes. The generic conventions used in each text varied within and between the texts and included non-technical narrative and instructional texts.

'Scientificness'

Different forms of schooled knowledge draw on different meaning-making resources and have preferred relations with different genres. This is something that students have to understand and they have to make decisions about what genre to use. These decisions will probably differ between the English classroom and the science classroom. When producing a text, whatever the subject area, students need to adopt a stance to the task, to choose a 'voice' in which to write to the reader. Much has been written on how school science genres are realized linguistically through the complex notion of 'voice', assumed knowledge, starting point and, more concretely, linguistic factors such as terminology, tense, genre and layout format of the text (Myers, 1990; Halliday and Martin, 1993; Lemke, 1998).

There are a number of ways of looking at what a teacher might regard as 'best' in relation to written texts produced by students in a classroom. In the case of school science, 'best' is usually considered to be what most approximates to the recontextualized genres of school science. There are clear protocols on how to 'be scientific': how to look through a microscope, how to observe a phenomenon and how to produce a written text. Science teachers are likely to have expectations of how 'scientificness' is best realized linguistically. These might include conventions such as using the genre of procedure rather than of narrative, use of the passive voice, use of the present tense, use of specialized terminology, a high degree of nominalization, and following a specific format in layout, the kind of distinctions which mark the formal boundaries between forms of schooled knowledge.

In comparison, the visual realization of 'scientificness' has received less attention in educational research and the school curriculum. Decisions on framing can be understood as an attempt to encode the scientific process of seeing through a microscope, each of which suggests depiction of different realities. For example, the students' drawings discussed in this paper are framed differently: some have a circular frame, others a rectangular frame. This use of frame introduces the idea that in science a different concept of reality (i.e. scientific realism) underlies the textual modality (Kress and van Leeuwen, 1996). The orientation of a visual text can be understood by attending to visual semiotic structures such as composition, the frame of an image, salience (via features such as size, colour and placement in the image space), materiality and modality (i.e. colour, contextualization, representation and depth).

Students use visual and linguistic conventions to produce texts which represent and mediate their experiences of learning and of 'being scientific' in different ways. In turn, these choices mediate students' success or failure in the science classroom. Here we focus on how two students' texts mediated the construction of themselves and their texts through the resources made available to them in the science classroom. We discuss how the expressions of 'scientificness' in the visual and written elements of the students' texts are not necessarily in parallel and how a student may realize different aspects of 'scientific-ness' visually and linguistically. By taking a multimodal approach we suggest that a text which ostensibly looks like it has failed to represent 'scientificness' linguistically may successfully realize it visually.

'Scientificness' via the visual

If one focuses on the written elements of the text produced by Student A (Figure 5.1 below) it appears to fall outside the conventions of a scientific text. The description of 'what I did' is a simple narrative rather than the genre of 'procedure' preferred in school science. The voice in the writing is personal rather than distant and agent-less. The agent of the action is present and her accomplice is named. The narrative begins with an account of the collection of the equipment at the beginning of the experiment. Student A assumes the need to explain everything to the reader who thus becomes an observer.

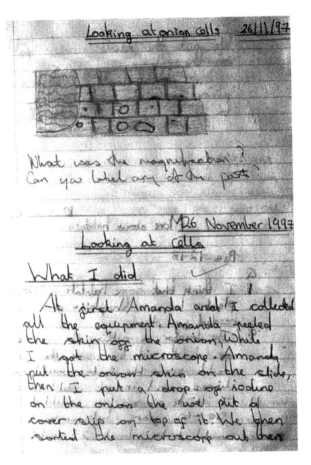

FIGURE 5.1 *Student A's text.*

The narrator expresses her feelings about the experiment which, combined with the use of past tense declaratives, turns the text into a relaying of a particular known event. The voice is confessional (e.g. 'it was interesting to look at and draw') while the genre conventions are reminiscent of a personal account such as a diary. The use of the past tense is significant as it is outside the conventions for this writing in the science classroom (and the worksheet models presented by the teacher). Through her writing Student A tells the story of what she and another student did and how she felt about it. She involves the reader in her experience of the lesson. The use of narrative incorporates a sense of action and the experience of the experiment (e.g. the use of terminology focused on the experience of using the microscope). Student A's use of narrative is close to a transformation of the 'scientificness' of fact, i.e. she may have used narrative to provide a factual account within a genre not preferred in the classroom. Nonetheless, the writing expresses Student A's understanding of what a scientific text should be, one that is different from the teacher's.

By contrast we suggest that the image in Student A's text does express a complex understanding of what a scientific text should be. While the written narrative in the text attempts to represent 'What I did', the image is a conceptual representation of a generalization of what was observed. The image draws on scientific codes of representation (e.g. the waving lines in the left section of the image and the lack of depth) to realize an abstracted account of cells. The drawing appears to be primarily concerned with the idea of regularity and sameness: a visual search for and presentation of 'scientificness' as a generalized pattern of meaning. The distinctly different pattern of the air bubble (the circle on the left of the image) and of the cells visually marks their difference (although Student A actually thought the air bubble was a part of the cell rather than an irregularity).

As Student A looked through the microscope in the lesson she said, 'It looks like a brick wall'. This analogy is also apparent in her drawing of the cells. She applied the metaphor of a brick wall, suggested in the worksheet and implied in the teacher's verbal analogy with building blocks, and reproduced it in the visual mode. The metaphor focused on the positive elements of regularity and uniformity of cells and embodies the relationship of the part (the cell or brick) to the whole (the onion or the brick wall). A brick wall is a familiar thing in an urban environment and the familiarity implied by the student's analogy comments on its everydayness: cells are everywhere.

The rectangular framing of the image of onion cells indicates that what is important is not a representation of everything that can be seen through the microscope (the eye's view) but a selection of this. The frame of the image is abstracted from what was seen. The aperture of the microscope lens is not represented and the image is of a generalized section of the cells. Student A's decision to use a rectangular frame offers a view in which the microscope which mediates between the student's eye and reality has been left out. Within the visual abstraction of the cell it is perhaps interesting that Student A represented the air bubble on the left of the image, that is, that the empirical is read as reality. In the same image the shading, use of colour (a pale green-yellow wash) and the level of detail represented in the image is suggestive of a naturalistic account. The combination of scientific and naturalistic codes in the image in Student A's drawing expresses the complexity of entering a new school genre and the relatively new concept of 'scientificness' for students in Year 7. This merging of genre conventions is also evident in the worksheets provided by the teacher.

The format of the text, in particular the order of image and writing, appears to be significant in the emerging notion of 'scientificness' in Student A's text. The image is arguably the most salient element of the text. Image and writing are presented under different titles and the date heads each section of the text. The image is titled 'Looking at onion cells'. The writing is titled 'Looking at cells' and 'What I did'. The image and the writing are presented as two distinct parts of the same text. Their separation is further emphasized by a line dividing them (the fact that they are on the same page maintains their connection as one textual unit).

The separation of the visual and written elements of the text marks a shift from the abstract (visual) to the specific concrete actions located in the student's personal experience (written). The layout of the text marks a separation between the result of the experiment and the process. We suggest that through the student's use of layout she has transformed the linguistically structured notion of text embedded in the teacher's instructions into a visually structured notion of a text. The semiotic meaning of linguistic texts is underpinned by the temporal dimension of writing: the meaning structure of earlier and later is an important dimension in the presentation and establishment of the meaning of linguistic texts. The linguistically given notion of text suggested by the teacher (realized by his instruction to write in the top half of the page and draw in the bottom half) used this temporal dimension to establish 'method' as coming first and 'result' as coming later, i.e. the format of the text is within the generic scientific convention of method (the written is first) followed by result (the visual is later). We suggest that Student A employed the meaning-structures of a visually structured text and used the spatial dimensions of visual meaning-making and, in so doing, transformed this generic convention into an alternative scientific convention: the result (visual) as idealized followed by the process (written) as real.

Discussion with Student A identified that her concern for neatness (which we interpret as a concern with space and order) was a salient influence on her text production. This concern can be seen as a form of discrimination of what is essential, which itself could be argued to be an aspect of scientificness. In other words, the text cleverly accommodates both the student's concerns and the teacher's focus on the separation of the processes of seeing and doing. This offers one explanation of her use of the visual to describe a generalized specific event (looking at onion cells), and writing to describe a more personal general process (looking at cells). Student A used different modes to realize different functions which she considered to be important in the production of a text and used the visual mode primarily to convey being scientific.

'Scientificness' via the linguistic

Student B has realized the key conventions of a scientific text in the written element of the text (Figure 5.2). The voice is impersonal, the agent is unnamed and imperatives on how to recreate the experiment are addressed to an unspecified reader. Because of its unexpressed addressee, the imperative has a generalizing effect. It conveys 'what one should do in order to achieve what I did'. The effacing of the speaker as much as that of the addressee is part of the attempt to produce the writing as factual and objective (as modelled in the worksheet). Through the use of linguistic devices that make things seem obvious or naturally present the writing embodies the assumption that the writer and reader share the same knowledge.

The absent writer serves to absent the audience: they are nowhere addressed and yet they are assumed to be completely known and therefore present in every facet of the language (Kress, 1994). The voice of the writing serves to distance Student B from

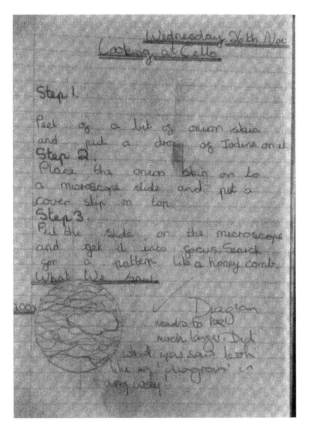

FIGURE 5.2 *Student B's text.*

the experience of the experiment. In contrast to her excited exclamations in the classroom, she chose in her writing to place herself outside of what she did. The writing is an instructive account. Through the use of imperatives in her writing she implicitly constructs the writer of the account as instructor and the reader as actor – rather than as observer, as in the other texts which we discuss. The writing presents a step-by-step process of how to repeat the experiment. It presents Student B as having passed through the experience of the experiment and able to describe how to re-create it. In presenting herself as outside the experiment giving directions, Student B's writing embodies what is best in school science.

In contrast, the visual element of her text is perhaps the most personal and least scientific. The teacher's somewhat desperate comment on Student B's image, 'Did what you saw look like my "diagram" in any way?' suggests that he would agree with this assessment. The image lacks colour and possesses a flatness, both of which are suggestive of an abstract representation moving more toward a scientific code than a naturalistic one. The image has a circular frame which was tentatively drawn with a compass which may itself be suggestive of a tension between the certainty of a mechanically produced circle and the hesitancy of the maker. The circular frame of the image is a convention generally used to encode the experience of seeing through a microscope. Its effect is to make the tool which leads to the representation (the microscope) a part of the representation.

Where another student's use of the circular framing device was imbued with 'scientificness' through a visual reference to the equipment of science, we suggest that Student B's use of the circular frame combines with the pattern created by the organic flow of the lines in the image to suggest the experience of looking. Student B's image realizes a sensory or aesthetic code focusing on the emotion and effect of the event rather than a scientific code. The image realizes Student B's involvement and excitement. The interest in the sensory is carried by Student B's analogy of 'a wavy weave – in and out of each other in our microscopes' when talking about her text. The image is represented beneath the heading 'What We Saw' and the heading for the writing is 'Looking at Cells'. These titles suggest that the agency involved in the visual experience of looking at the cells is different to the agency involved in making them visible. Through the writing Student B transformed her experience of doing the experiment into a generalized set of actions while through her image she asserts her individual experience of seeing the cells.

In Student B's text the separation between image and writing is less marked than in the texts of Student A. The writing and the image in Student B's text are presented under two headings, although the heading for the image follows on from and appears to merge with the writing in the previous section. The image is partially integrated with the heading 'What We Saw' in that the top of the image is inserted between the first two words. The image thus provides visual evidence of the experience described in Student B's writing. By following the teacher's instructions on the order of the image and written elements of the text (writing first, followed by image) Student B produced a text that exists within the meaning structures of a linguistic text. As a consequence the writing has the meaning status of first = earlier, and the image has the status of what resulted later – the sensory experience as an outcome of the procedure.

Summary: Achieving 'scientificness'

Our analysis shows that the students' texts vary significantly and suggest that both students imported different elements from the teacher's instructions, talk, the worksheets and their experience of the experiment. Table 5.1 below summarizes the dimensions of the semiotic variation between the two texts described above.

The students were all involved in the serious task of producing a text appropriate to a science lesson and each found different ways of realizing 'scientificness' in their texts. The process of producing scientific drawings appeared to us to be about the students' process of learning what to see and the transition from looking within the frame of naturalistic realism to that of scientific realism, which is in fact a hyperreality that gives visual form to things not usually seen.

This transition is about the process of negotiation and selection by students of what it is important to include and to make visible in their representations. In this way the texts reflect a sense of each of the students' identity in this respect: who, how and what each is meant to imagine herself to be when writing her text in this new domain of science and its new demands of being scientific, which demands forms of representing the world in which what happened once should be described so that it can be made to happen again. That is, they reflect the ability of each student to envisage the experiment as repeatable.

For us, the texts are not, mainly, evidence of the students' ability but of the consequences of the students' differently interested use of genre and mode resources: their quite different emerging sense of 'scientificness' and of its expression. The students' experiences were mediated through their use of image and writing in the texts.

Table 5.1 Criteria for 'scientificness'

Criterion	Text 1	Text 2
Visual representation	scientific – abstract	sensory – aesthetic
Frame	rectangular	circular
Air bubble	represented distinct – exaggerated	incorporated within pattern
Metaphor	brick wall	wavy weave
Use of colour	yellow-green	pencil drawing
Written genre	narrative – journal	procedure
Agent/pronoun	named/I	absent
Order of modes	image writing	writing image
Epistemological meaning of text	image – idealized result writing – real process	writing – first process image – sensory outcome
Relationship between visual and written	most distinct	partially merged

The visual and written elements of the texts contributed differently to the realization of 'being scientific' and to the experience and meaning of the experiment for each. We suggest that the differences between the texts can be explained by seeing them as the product of the different stances each student adopted to the recording of their experience of learning, and to how they saw the protocol of 'being scientific' (as summarized in Table 5.1).

There are a number of ways of looking at what a teacher might regard as 'best' in relation to the texts produced by students in a classroom. In the case of school science 'best' is usually considered to be what most approximates being scientific. There are clear protocols on how to be scientific: how to look through a microscope, observe a phenomenon and produce a text. Science teachers are likely to have (implicitly held) expectations of how scientificness is best realized linguistically and visually. However, the production and assessment of the visual in students' texts is more marginal than is the linguistic, which is often not available as explicitly articulated knowledge within the school. The visual is seldom seen to carry meaning beyond being that of an illustration of the accompanying writing. Yet it is clear that in science education as elsewhere the visual is moving to equality in many instances with the written mode. This is evident in the shift from the written to the visual in education textbooks. This has resulted in the different expressions and reshapings of knowledge we discussed in the preceding chapter. Students need to be able to read the visual as meaningful. The visual now functions as a representational mode and it is a fundamentally important resource in the classroom. It highlights the importance of taking students' production of images seriously.

The realization by students of the representational requirements of scientific texts may be masked by those who presently set the agendas for school education, because of the high social and cultural value placed on linguistic resources within education and traditional linguistic approaches to texts in the classroom. A multimodal approach draws attention to the joint significance of visual and written elements of texts and to their distinctively different contributions to the meaning of a text. We are not suggesting that the realization of meanings through speech or writing is no longer important but that the visual is also important. Meaning-making, teaching and learning can no longer be considered as purely linguistic accomplishments.

6

Written genres and the transformation of multimodal communication: Students' signs as evidence of learning

Introduction

The texts discussed in this chapter were written as homework following a series of lessons on blood circulation (the first lesson in the series is discussed in Chapter 2). The teacher asked the students to write a 'story' about the blood's journey around the body from the point of view of a blood cell. The first point to make is that the students' stories varied, providing us with a powerful example of how seeing and learning are different for different students. In other words, the texts offer some evidence of the different possibilities for understanding and transforming signs through their selection, adaptation and reproduction. Our analysis explored a range of elements and concepts within the students' texts, including centrality and direction; the introduction, classification and construction of entities; students' use of voice and agency within the texts; the use of format, layout, style and the genre conventions used; and the different discourses informing the texts (e.g. social, biological and medical). Here we discuss just one key idea from our analysis of a sample of the students' texts: the relationship between multimodality and genre.

The teacher used a range of semiotic resources during the lesson. However, when he set the homework task, he explicitly limited the mode in which the task should be undertaken to written language. The homework therefore required the students to translate the teacher's multimodal messages/signs into written language (although some read this as freedom to draw images as well). We were interested in the different ways in which students transformed the teacher's multimodal representation of the circulation of the blood (information from the teacher's speech, his use of images and his manipulation of the model) into a written text.

The students' texts used a range of different genre conventions. They needed to adopt a stance to their story, to choose a voice with which to speak to the reader. Our point here is not that the texts should have shared the features of one genre but to show that the students use generically specific conventions which work to present their experience of learning in different ways. It is a common-sense observation that people use language differently in different situations. Halliday uses the term 'register' to refer to the systematic links between the organization of language and the organization of the context (Halliday and Martin, 1993). In contrast to Martin (1993), our interest is not focused on the identification and classification of genre models but on knowing what generic conventions were taken up by teachers and students and trying to understand why. In order to do this we employ Kress's broad concept of genre (Kress, 1993) as a device to analyse the stability and dynamic variation between the texts introduced by the teacher and those produced by the students (Kress, 1993). We see genre as an aid to explaining the process of the selection of the text and of the production of texts, rather than a way of describing the text as a product, which is not our primary interest here (see Hodge and Kress, 1988).

Our approach does not impose genre models on our data for the purpose of classification. It does maintain our focus on the dynamic process of textual production and helps us to emphasize the work of students as active decision-makers who make choices which realize their stance in the production of texts. Of course we are interested in focusing on genre as a matter of ability and knowledge. Importantly for our purpose now we are interested in the semiotic affordances of different genres because it is these which are brought into play when students select and condense elements of the ensembles of multimodality into the representational possibilities of a genre.

Below we discuss the decisions students made in producing their text in relation to a number of key aspects: voice (active or passive), tense (past or present), 'key players', the format of presentation, and style of the text. Genre features may be one resource available to students with which to transform ensembles of multimodal communication into a written text. We might then view aspects of the genre as traces or echoes of the multimodal environment.

Some of the genre conventions used by the students reproduced those used by the teacher through the series of lessons. They included fairy tale, scientific report and investigative journalism. Other genres which appear to have been introduced by the students from other sources included Dear Diary, video diary, fantasy-nightmare, Captain's log, our own correspondent from the front line and spy-action movie. The students' notion of a story and the components they thought of as a part of a good story bring us into the realm of their interests. Analysis of the genre conventions in the texts offers us and the students' teacher a way into the world of their interests. A brief example and discussion of four of these genres is offered below.

Spy-action movie genre

One student's text introduces elements of the genre spy-action movie including missions, mystery and dual identity (discussed later), and cleverly signals this by echoing the stereotype 'My name is Bond, James Bond':

My name is Blood, James Blood! My mission is first to deliver oxygen to body cells then carry on and after four months I'll next become a white blood cell and get the job at beating up some nasty germs and viruses (such is life).

This genre presents a format which readily focuses on the action of a particular hero or anti-hero, in this case James Blood. The genre gives more weight to what James Blood does than how he feels about it. The genre markers of spy-action movie enable the student to attend to the difference between red and white blood cells. In the text this is achieved through the duality of James Blood's life, his 'red life' and his 'white life'. Duality is often associated with spies or action heroes (such as Clark Kent-Superman, Bruce Wayne-Batman). The good-natured, bumbling buffoon, the nice guy, the hyper-normal guy transforms himself into the powerful, possibly violent (but well-intentioned) hero.

In this student's text the red blood cell is a good-natured person who carries out his tasks without real complaint:

> After collecting the oxygen I come along a tube to another chamber at the heart where (yes, again) get squeezed, this time round the whole of the body!

In his text, the student constructs the white blood cell as a superhero:

> There might be fewer of us but we are bigger, stronger and better.

This hero graduates from the Academy of the Heart to 'patrol' and 'guard' the human. A comparison of the student's visual representations of the red and white blood cells supports this idea of transformation and duality (Figure 6.1).

The genre enables the student to focus on duality and action and to transform the teacher's fairy tale analogy (discussed earlier) into a modern-day version. Here it is important to note that it is the genre that drives the facts. Red blood cells do not turn into white blood cells.

But the genre works better if they do. So the 'fact' that they do is invented by the student.

FIGURE 6.1 *A comparison of the images of red and white blood cells from a student's text.*

Fairy-tale genre

Elements of fairy-tale genre conventions were used in another text, including the opening sentence 'Once upon a time . . .', the symbolic reference to Little Red Riding Hood and the use of a name which points to the character's nature, Herman Growch.

> Once upon a time there lived a little blood cell. His name was Robert the red blood cell. Robert lived inside a boy called Herman Growch and one day Robert decided to do something different for a change . . .

The genre markers of a fairy tale continue throughout the student's story, including the statement towards the end which is a transformation of the traditional fairy-tale ending 'ever after':

> . . . and that is what he did every minute of every day for the rest of his life.

This text deals with a key aspect of the teacher's construction of the blood circulation – cyclical movement. The reference to time and the implicit reference to monotony in the above statement, and perhaps the general cultural resource of eternity, help to carry the notion of a cycle in the text. The use of a chronological narrative format provides a framework for the direction of the journey of the blood. It goes from the lungs to the small intestine, then on to 'every cell in the body', finally to the heart, and 'back around'.

The teacher's descriptions of the process of circulation included the naming of the body parts involved in the process and focused on the heart as the key actor in the process, the blood being the goal of this action. In the student's text the roles of the blood and the heart have been transformed. The red blood cell is the main actor in the story. He has a name, Robert (and thereby a gender), he has a home, he makes decisions, he has a physical and an emotional life. The only other actor in the story is the heart which 'pumped him back around'. The sense that it is the heart which pumps the blood is lost in the main. The blood is transformed from the passive entity constructed by the teacher into a self-motivated agent.

Again, the genre requires this: it is one of its affordances. The players in the students' texts are selected from those introduced by the teacher – the lungs, small intestine, heart and every cell in the body. The kidneys, liver and the detail of the heart's structure are not included. Perhaps this highlights the student's focus on the *role* of the blood and its agentive action rather than treating the blood as a passive entity. In other words, the blood can be shown as active in the process of getting and taking sugar and oxygen, and in relation to the lungs, small intestine, heart and body cells, but *not* in relation to the kidneys and liver where it is 'cleaned'. So the transformative work of the student recasts the epistemological framework from purpose to purposive action. The teacher presented the blood as passive (acted on) but this has for him a global purpose. In the student's text the purpose of blood is localized (in the cell) and is transformed into action. The organs are transformed into *sites of action* (places) or *helpers of action* (the heart). The fairy tale genre enables the student to focus on one key agent (Robert the red blood cell) and his adventures in his world (Herman Growch).

In lesson four the teacher used an analogy drawn from the genre of fairy tales. He suggested that the students think of the body as 'a castle', the white blood cells as 'knights' and viruses as an 'invading king's army'. Perhaps the teacher's metaphor informed this student's text. Whatever the source of the genre, the fairy tale provides a convention where the incredible is treated as real. It offers a ready context for the imaginative act of the student – being a blood cell. The use of the body as a metaphor for society, the ability to alter (or disregard) size and the personification or animation of entities are all well-established conventions within the fairy tale. Within the tradition of fairy tales many questions can remain unanswered and remain unproblematic, requiring little detail and attention from the student – anything can happen. At the same time both fairy tale and spy-action movie make available quite clearly articulated structures which are drawn on to provide the structure for the organization of knowledge.

Personal account genre

The students' texts include three styles of personal account: 'Dear Diary', video diary and 'Captain's log'. The genres of diary and log are concerned with time, while all the diaries, though not perhaps the log, can deal with the emotional, personal experience of the everyday. The decision to use this genre can be seen as a response to the teacher's focus on cyclical movement, his personification of the blood cells and the repositioning of the students throughout the lessons. The choice of the format suggests the students' interest is in the personal, emotional aspects of (the blood cell's) life, especially as this is an account of a 'journey'.

Within the conventional Dear Diary format seconds rather than days are used as the markers of the cycle of time. The address is first person and there are fresh entries for each time slot. Similar conventions of the personal account inform other students' texts. In this example the format is modernized in the style of a video diary: the narrator addresses us directly. She introduces herself to us, telling us her name, her job and what this involves, and how she feels about it:

> Hello my name is Roxane the red blood cell.
> My job is to keep Timinisha alive and full of energy . . .
> I only live for 4 months. But I don't care if I die as long as I die with dignity of helping.

The Captain's log account can be seen as a sort of masculinized version of Dear Diary. The narrator is in charge, he makes a record of the facts.

This account uses the days of the week to provide the sense of a cycle:

> Tue: Today a disease called chicken Pox got into the body. We are fighting like mad to get this out. It'll take a day or too.
>
> [and later]
>
> Sat: We're all getting very tired and sleepy 'yawn' and ah . . . Shame we can't live to Sunday.

However, the cycle is not completed in this last text as the cells all die before the week is out. Perhaps this is a form of tacit non-compliance with the task, or maybe it just demonstrates the student's keen interest in death.

In these personal accounts the process of how events come about is absent or backgrounded. What is foregrounded is the author's response to the events, not the events themselves. When events or information were focused on, as in the second text discussed in this section, the narrator's emotions were usually interwoven:

> I collect oxygen from the lungs. I always have to take my A-Z because it's so easy to get lost in there. It is also very windy. . . . I go to the heart to be pumped so that I will be able to go quickly around the body. The surrounding is very hot. It is rather uncomfortable actually because you get squeezed through . . . I do get rather bored for doing the same thing everyday.

The focus on emotions and personal experience in the diary format is also used to transform physical issues into social issues. For example, in the first text discussed the size of the cells is transformed into a metaphor for social class through references to living conditions and used to evoke class solidarity – 'there are millions of us':

> Dear Diary, I am currently in the lungs, it is terribly cramped in here as the capillaries are tiny and there are millions of us.

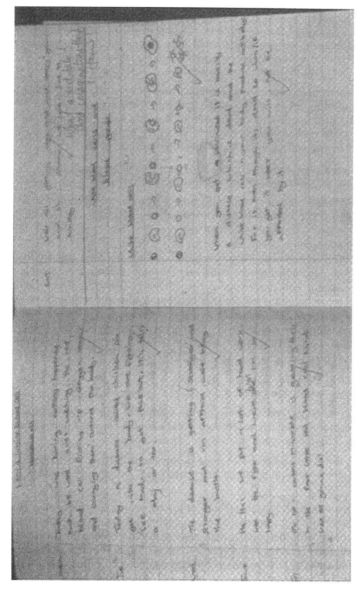

FIGURE 6.2 *'Dear Diary' format of student's text.*

Rather than reporting the individual experience of a cell, the text written in the style of Captain's log focused on large-scale emotions and issues – conflict, glory and the drama of foreseen disaster. His personal account is elevated to that of a historical record.

The different styles of personal account used by the students worked to encode different social relationships between the reader and the narrator (the teacher and the student). The Dear Diary genre encodes an intimate relationship between reader and author – we are her best friend. The video diary format offers an intimate but public relationship – we can all be her friend. The Captain's log places us in a more distanced relation to the narrator – either as his or her superior, or in respect to time.

Fantasy-nightmare genre

Other students' texts conjure up the emotional panic of a nightmare through the use of agent-less action, the narrator's lack of control in the story and horror-genre references. For example:

> Inside me I could feel the sugar and oxygen burning and producing energy. Something was coming behind me, It was getting faster and faster.

In this text each sentence shifts to a new setting or experience. This constant shifting provides a sense of movement, and this movement combines with the fantasy–nightmare genre to produce a sense of the blood cells' actions as compelled rather than voluntary. The text reproduces the passiveness of the blood apparent in the lessons – the blood circulates, but it does so because of something else (the heart). This contrasts with the transformation of purpose in the fairy-tale genre into purposive action. Here it is all happening but if there is a purpose, the cell does not know about it. At times the heart is the explicit agent in the text, at other points it is the absent agent, the 'something'. The heart plays the role of the ghoul:

> Then I was being pushed right up to the kidneys . . . I was then pushed on to the lungs . . .

The textbook used by the teacher makes a visual reference to horror movies in the form of a vampire which may be one source of the student's references. The use of this genre focuses on the sensory experience of the blood's journey around the body. The organs (with the exception of the heart) mentioned in the story provide a setting for the action. The artery, small intestine and lungs are almost incidental to the real event: movement. In this way the centrality of the heart in the story is established. The cycle of movement described in the text provides a nightmarish transformation of the teacher's focus on movement and direction in the lesson. What appears to be important to the student who made this text is not the specific direction or order of the movement of the blood but the sense of speed and compulsion.

This text is one of three that includes images. The images are separate from and come after the text. The function of the first image (Figure 6.3) appears to be to locate the organs mentioned in the story within the context of the human body. The image also introduces the wind pipe which connects the internal process of the blood circulation with elements external to the body: blood circulation requires oxygen and oxygen is in the air. In this way the image provides a context for the circulation of the blood beyond the body.

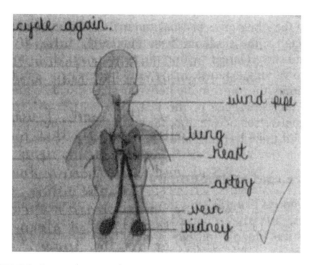

FIGURE 6.3 *Image from student's text.*

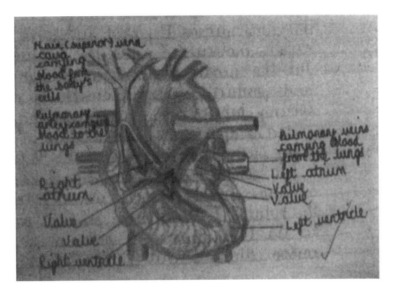

FIGURE 6.4 *Detailed labelled drawing of the heart from student's text.*

The second image (Figure 6.4) provides a detailed labelled drawing of the heart, almost as a detail to the first image. The centrality of the heart in the story is confirmed through this detailed image. The visual representation of direction by the arrows and the notation of the process included in the labels gives a visual and written summary of the process.

Although some students' texts maintained a stable set of genre markers and stayed largely within the mode of writing (using the mode of layout to varying extents), many were multigeneric and multimodal texts. At times the movement between genres within the same text weakened the coherence of the text. One text moved between four different genres: science fiction, fairy tale, confessional statements of the diary and the adventure and drama of a soap opera.

Genre and multimodality

Different genres, like different modes, have particular constraints and affordances, and they enabled the students to focus on different aspects of the blood's journey around the body, and to introduce different interests. The students' genre choices and shifts within their texts also enabled them to encode different interests and different social relationships between themselves as author-narrator and the teacher-reader. This encoding occurred in the layout of the page and the use of space and type, images and text.

The students transformed the teacher's multimodal ensemble, his construction of the entity 'blood circulation', through image, gesture, action, manipulation of the model and his use of his body and speech into written (and to a lesser extent, visual) texts. We have shown above how genre played a key role in the reorganization of this transformation of meanings across mode. Through attending to concepts such as direction, agency and voice we have argued that genre can be read in the students' texts as a trace or echo of the multimodal environment of the science classroom.

Some of the genre conventions used by students were reproduced or transformed from the teacher's communicative actions, others were imported from elsewhere. The genres chosen by the students structured the focus of their texts to a greater or lesser extent. That is, some genres make it easier to focus on a particular aspect of the lesson than others. The genres chosen by the students can be seen as their attempt to bring in their different interests, for instance, the genres introduced the dynamics of action in different ways. Some texts brought in a sense of action through references to multimedia formats (e.g. spy–action movie, CD-ROM). Others introduced the idea of action and movement by telling their stories against a backdrop of the cycle of time in the form of a diary, which also served to provide a sense that the 'life' of a blood cell is a monotonous one. In some texts it seemed clear that it was the selection of 'facts' that led to the choice of genre which then drove the story. In other cases it seemed that the writer's interests were first and foremost on the genre and its affordances which then led to selections and organizations of the 'content' in line with the affordances of the genre. In those cases the texts were genre driven.

The voices which students chose to use in their texts varied. Some students spoke directly to the reader. Some students created a narrator to speak on their behalf. Others used a confessional format, an intimate voice, such as Dear Diary. Through their choice of voice, format and the focus of their texts the students created different degrees of distance between themselves as the author of their text and the reader, ostensibly the teacher (the students did not know that we would read their stories). The scientific reporter and investigative journalist became authoritative experts on the life experience of the cell, and the reader became his or her audience. In contrast, the confessor in Dear Diary let us into her world rather than the world of another and we became her friend. But to read the Captain's log would usually require us to be his or her superior.

We can view genre conventions as an important mechanism, first for getting started on the task of writing the story set by the teacher and second as a way of keeping going with the task. We can perhaps imagine the student's task in the following way: (i) What do I want to say? (ii) Which genre gives me a starting point that will best do this? Which fits what I want to say? (iii) What happens next? If we imagine the work of the student in this way it raises the question of what is driving the story – genre or 'fact'? If the student's text is genre-driven then the question of 'What next?' is answered by assuming that the genre expects X-fact so I must find or invent X-fact. If the text is fact-driven, it follows that the response to the question 'What next?' is most likely to be 'Now I must say Y-fact. Can I fit Y-fact into the existing genre I have chosen?'. If so, we suggest that the student will continue in the same genre. If not, it is likely that the student will change genre. We therefore speculate that a student's frequent change in genre may indicate his or her greater interest in factuality than in imaginative and generic coherence.

7

Materiality as an expression of learning

Introduction

In this chapter we focus on four three-dimensional models of a plant cell produced by Year 7 students in a girls' school in London. The models (Figures 7.2 to 7.5) were produced as homework following an introductory lesson on cells. The students were given a week to make them. The question raised for us (and the teacher) by these models was what the models mean for learning.

Transformations: New signs

We analyse the students' models of a cell as textual objects, signs of their interested activity and as a way to bridge multimodal texts and practices. We look at how the students used and appropriated the resources made available to them (school science styles, conventions, analogy and metaphor, and materiality) for their own meaning-making purposes in order to express their interests.

The page of the textbook (Figure 7.1) was offered as a key resource by the teacher. It can be read as the authoritative sign 'cells', the knowledge at issue in its canonical form. The students' models can then be seen as transformations of this sign and as new signs. In the textbook two types of cell were represented, a cheek cell and a pond weed cell. For both representations, image was the foregrounded mode in the form of a photograph and a diagram, with writing used for

6.1   Cells

Before the photographs of the cells shown below were taken, a dye was put on the cells. This helps to show up the different parts of each cell. The photographs were then taken with a camera fitted to a microscope:

Cheek cell

Pond weed cell

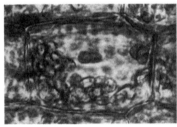

This is a photo of a cheek cell. The inside of your cheek is made up of many of these cells. In fact, your whole body is made up of millions and millions of tiny living cells joined together.
A diagram to help you see the main parts of the cheek cell is given below:

This is a photo of a cell from pond weed. The weed is made up of millions of tiny living cells, too.
A diagram to help you see the main parts of the pond weed cell is given below:

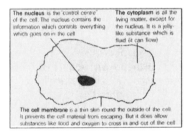

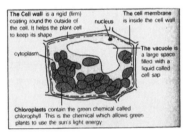

1   Why is the nucleus called the 'control centre' of the cell? ▲
2   What is the cytoplasm? What is it like? ▲
3   What is a cell vacuole? ▲
4   a) What do chloroplasts contain? ▲
    b) Why is this important? (Look at page 27 if you need help!)
5   Pick out the three parts which are found both in the cheek cell and in the pond weed cell (and in most other cells, too!).
6   **Try to find out:** when cells were discovered, and by whom.

Did you know?

• The cell membrane is only 0.000 01 mm thick.
• Animal cells don't have chloroplasts. They don't have cell walls either.

FIGURE 7.1 *Textbook page on cells (Alan Frasier and Ian Gilchrist, Starting Science, Book 1, Oxford University Press, 1996). (Reproduced by permission of Oxford University Press)*

a variety of purposes ranging from label to paragraph. The students' models are a transformation of the textbook sign 'cell' on two levels: that of mode and that of elements/content.

At the level of mode the students' models transformed the sign 'cell' as presented in the textbook from a written and visual two-dimensional representation into a predominantly visual three-dimensional representation. This shift brought different representational potentials. For example, in the models the students used texture and shape in ways that are not possible (or practical) in a textbook. Water was used to represent the liquid in the vacuole, and a piece of sponge to represent the nucleus.

The expansion from the affordances of the two-dimensional page to those of a three-dimensional model made available different potentials for representing the elements and the relations between them. The three-dimensional models afforded the potential for more complex spatial arrangements between the elements than the textbook image (e.g. layering, and depth). In school science, cells are commonly interpreted by students as flat, since this is how they appear through a microscope. The models overcame this common interpretation of cells by presenting the space occupied by the cell as three-dimensional.

The students' models transformed the textbook sign by selecting, adapting and transforming elements of the visually and verbally represented cell, and transforming the relations between elements of the cell. The students transformed the spatial arrangement of the elements and the colour of some of them to make them more salient and to bring them into prominence.

> I: So is your model like a model of the drawing?
> S1: Well this cytoplasm went down like that and the nucleus was a really round circle in the middle and the vacuole was up here, so we changed it round.
> S2: And we didn't put the cytoplasm where it was in the book.
> S1: It isn't really the same as in the book.
> I: Right.
> S2: But we did take ideas from the book.
> S1: And, erm, in the book the nucleus was black.
> S2: So we thought we'd do it red.

In the textbook the two types of cell were presented as visually distinct via the compositional means of the page – the animal cell on the left, the plant cell on the right and the use of different colours to represent each cell type (blue for animal cell and green and yellow for plant cell). Some of the students merged elements from these two cell types to create a model of a new generalized sign 'cell'. Comparison of the students' models of a cell shows that each model/sign:

1   was a transformation of the textbook sign 'cell'.

2   used different representational resources in the semiotic modes available to the students to make the sign.

3   reflected the cognitive decisions involved in representing a cell as a three-dimensional sign.

In our analysis here we explore the models as expressions of learning in order to demonstrate that the transformative processes in which the students engaged (e.g. their selection of resources, their decisions in arranging the elements in relation to one another) required them to engage with kinds of thinking and learning which a purely linguistic task would not have required.

Reality in the science classroom

The criteria for the visual representation of truth are established by different social groups for the contexts in which they interact. These criteria, developed out of the central values, beliefs and social needs of these groups, act as relatively reliable guides to the truth or factuality of messages (Hodge and Kress, 1988; Kress and van Leeuwen, 1996). The students who made the models discussed in this chapter expressed the need for their models to relate to the 'real thing', to focus on and signal the criterial aspects of a cell, and to communicate meaning about the cell in particular ways. In the making of their models the students were engaged in the complex task of abstracting features of the entity 'cell' and presenting the abstraction as a likeness to the real thing. In part the students achieved this through their selection and arrangement of materials and imported objects – one part of their transformative action. In other words, texture, shape and colour were used as signifiers of meaning – a range of resources which were selected and arranged to create meanings of truth, fact, certainty and credibility. What the students considered 'real' was informed by the framing of the task within science education. We asked the students what they liked about each other's models and it was clear that 'reality' was a central attribute for many of them. Here are two representative comments from that background.

S2:   I like Stacey's [Figure 7.2] because it doesn't look quite the same, it's different actually when you hold it up to the light it looks like real.

I: What do you mean? What looks real about it?

S2:   Well it looks . . .

S3:   It's not, like, symmetrical like a lot of ours.

S2:   Hers looks, I don't know, like it's not planned and stuff.

S1:   It's sort of like it's natural.

S3:   It isn't put together and it's like really good.

I: When you say it doesn't look planned like yours, it looks natural, tell me a bit what you mean.

S2:   Erm, I mean like, . . . say it, erm, like . . . symmetrical and things are exactly the same, but hers is like different and . . . like erm, it's like, it's like, it's just like, like it's not planned or anything . . . like everything is different.

I: Yeah.

S1:   She has her own ideas, like we looked in a book and we thought, oh this must be like this, and oh the vacuole must be like this, whereas she thought, oh well let's, I think I'm not going to be like the rest, I'm going to change it and be different.

S2:   Like . . . she put the string through the sponge so it's quite different, 'cos we've all like tried to get it exactly the same as we saw in the books and that.

S1:   She painted it green and she's just left hers quite simply and that.

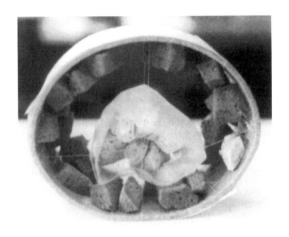

FIGURE 7.2 *Model 1 of a cell.*

In the context of science education, these students' sense of the characteristics of a visual representation of 'real' (and 'natural') appears to focus on two criteria: first, an absence of traces of the work involved in making the model (lack of planning and symmetry perceived as spontaneity, and therefore close to 'natural'), that is, an absence of the modeller guaranteeing absence of interference. Second, simplicity which belies the hard work involved in knowing what to leave out and what to put in, that is, how to abstract rather than simplify an object. In both cases human work is regarded as falsifying, as culture changing nature. We suggest that in an art classroom their sense of representations of reality would differ, perhaps focusing on a realism that stressed a likeness to nature. Making a model in art and in science both require labour, but the type of labour is different and the degree to which this labour is shown or allowed to be visible differs. Art is seen as showing the world as it is, science is seen as showing the world as it is known. In short, art is fact and science is interpretation: the reverse of the common-sense belief. The process of producing 'scientific' representations appeared to us to be about the students' process of learning what to see and the transition between looking from within the frame of naturalistic reality to seeing with the frame of scientific reality – a hyperreality that gives visual form to things not usually seen. This transition is the process of negotiation and selection by students of what it is important to them to include and to make visible in their representations.

Texture, shape and colour

The students used materials with different textures and colours to make their models of a cell. The students made selections from materials available to them (sometimes involving substantial negotiations with parents about the materials). Here we argue that the students' choice of texture and shape demanded thinking and decision-making in ways which a purely linguistic approach could not have.

In the textbook the cell wall was represented linguistically as a 'rigid (firm) coating [which] helps the plant cell to keep its shape' and visually by a thick black line. Each of the models used different thicknesses of cardboard, plastic and paper to represent the cell wall.

These materials were used to create a textual transformation of the wall as firm and smooth. In models 2 and 3 (Figures 7.3 and 7.4) a cardboard box represented the cell wall; in model 2 it was covered with paper and painted, the paint adding a powdery smoothness. The cell wall in model 4 (Figure 7.5) was made from papier-mâché over a plastic box placed on a polystyrene pizza base; the papier mâché was painted and covered with Sellotape to give a smooth varnished effect. The 'cell walls' were raised to enclose the elements of the cell, reflecting the common function of a wall. In the case of model 4, the student's use of colour (pale yellow), shape (circle) and texture (smooth, varnished) suggested a shell by analogy. Here the design of the cell walls captured the need to *look into the cell* to see the components. In model 1 (Figure 7.2) the student used a section of a thick oval cardboard tube to represent the cell wall. This model represented a more abstracted view of a cell and a different notion of containment. In model 4 (Figure 7.5) the student used a circular shape to represent the outside of the

FIGURE 7.3 *Model 2 of a cell*

FIGURE 7.4 *Model 3 of a cell.*

FIGURE 7.5 *Model 4 of a cell*

cell and a rectangular shape to represent the inner arrangement of elements. In this way she marked a clear distinction between inner and outer, which was further marked by her use of different colours to mark outer (yellow) and inner (green). This student's different use of shape and texture visually expressed notions of containment, transformed the two-dimensional representation in the textbook into a three-dimensional one and echoed Hooke's metaphor of cell wall (Hooke, 1667).

As in the textbook diagram (Figure 7.1), the cell membrane in each model was represented as different to the cell wall. In the textbook diagram the bold line for the wall contrasted with the lighter broken line representing the membrane. In contrast to the hard smoothness of the cell walls in the models, the cell membrane was represented as flimsy, shiny, crinkly and thin. Here the use of texture embodied the meaning of lived delicacy. Model 2 (Figure 7.3) used tissue paper, models 1 and 3 (Figures 7.2 and 7.4) used clingfilm, and model 4 (Figure 7.5) used the thin edge of a plastic box. In model 2 the cell membrane was represented from an aerial view. Oval leaf or petal shapes made out of tissue paper were glued (making the paper more transparent) onto a thin paper overhang around the top edge of the box. These materials realized students' understanding of how thin and delicate cell membranes are. In models 1 and 3 the use of clingfilm, and to a lesser extent the use of plastic in model 4, drew on the everyday function of these materials to express the function of the cell membrane to protect. In another model (not shown here) a raised line of cardboard dashes represented the cell wall – a direct translation/ transformation of the hesitancy of the line in the two-dimensional diagram. The students' choice of materials carried the meaning and function of delicacy in different ways and involved them in serious decisions around representation such as how to imbue specific qualities and meaning to a model cell through the affordances of materiality.

The nucleus was described in the textbook and by the students as the control centre of the cell. The importance of the nucleus signalled by this metaphor is represented in the use of texture and colour. In model 2 the structure of the nucleus is complex. It is constructed from a pink bath sponge (cut into a circle) covered with red tissue paper placed in a circle cut out from the raised base of the model. The students had used the sponge to make a *textural* analogy between the nucleus as control centre and the brain (as *sponge-like*, in a popular analogy based on 'absorbing knowledge'). The red tissue paper intensified the colour of the pink sponge – the increased saturation used to signify salience. Representing the nucleus as bouncy, spongy and red, the students had conferred on it the role of 'brain', thus confirming its centrality in the model.

S1: The nucleus is quite sort of like bouncy.

I: Why are they bouncy?

S2: I don't know.

S1: Well first we put in, erm, this pinkish sponge that she had.

S2: For scrubbing the body.

S1: And she cut a bit out and put it in, and I go and then we both decided to put tissue paper to make it.

S2: Because the sponge was bit dull.

S1: Yeah.

S2: The, erm, nucleus is the control centre of the cell.

I: The control centre?

S2: Yeah.

I: What does that mean?

S1: It's like the brain of the cell.

I: OK. What does it control?

S1: It just like controls.

S2: Everything inside the cell.

In model 3 (Figure 7.4), the solid heaviness of the stone used to represent the nucleus, its movement and the sound of its movement as it dragged or fell across the box of the model, drew attention to and highlighted the nucleus in a way that other elements did not. The size and colour (black) of the nucleus in model 4 (Figure 7.5) served to indicate its salience. In model 1 (Figure 7.2) the nucleus was represented as the control centre of the cell through the centrality of the arrangement of the elements within the oval cell wall. The tension of the string holding the elements together literally realized the central controlled meaning function of the nucleus. Through a variety of material means – texture, shape, heaviness and arrangement – the students visually and physically expressed the central role of the nucleus within their models.

The material realization of the chloroplasts in the models all reflected the students' sense of what the characteristics and the functions might be. The use of green in the models no doubt came from the textbook images of a pond weed cell but was transformed to a range of shades of green within a single model: possibly to show changing energy levels. The students' models transformed the shape of the chloroplasts in the diagram from the oval irregular shape to square chunks and petal shapes. The chloroplasts were represented as something 'wrapped', whether in tissue paper as in model 2 (Figure 7.1) or as sweet wrappers elsewhere. The function of the chloroplasts is to store the chemicals required for photosynthesis and the use of a wrapping appears to signify and imbue meanings of containment and storage while the texture of the material used in wrapping gave insight into what the students thought the texture and function of the 'skin' of the chloroplast might be.

Chloroplasts were also represented as leaf-like paper shapes painted shades of green as in model 3 (Figure 7.4). Here the use of texture and shape serves to highlight the organic result of the function of chloroplasts to keep leaves green. Additionally, they were represented as circular or square chunks of sponge painted green in models 1 and 4 (Figures 7.2 and 7.5). The students' decision to use sponge painted green appears to have been an attempt to draw on the analogy of sponge as container-absorber of greenness. The task engaged the students in new sign-making including the transformation of shape, colour and the introduction of texture to create visual representations of the function of the chloroplasts in a cell.

The vacuole was represented in the textbook as a lagoon-shaped space; in the models it was represented through a range of materials – in model 2 (Figure 7.3) by a plastic water bottle, in model 3 (Figure 7.4) by brown pencil lines on the base of the cardboard box. In model 4 (Figure 7.5), a curved shape made of newspaper, covered with paper and coloured in black and yellow lines, was used. Model 1 (Figure 7.2) used a thick bit of rubbery plastic with a powdery surface to represent the vacuole. Each of these textures refers to an aspect of the expression of liquid, employing materials in the most apt and plausible way to represent the students' interest. Model 2 used water as a direct representation of the movement of liquid. The arrangement of the elements in the inner base of model 3 was reminiscent of an aesthetic impression of a pond scene while the brown pencil lines are like a representation of the ripples in water. Model 4 used shape

Table 7.1 Students' textural representation of elements in
their models of a cell

		Texture		
Element	Model 1	Model 2	Model 3	Model 4
cell wall	smooth, firm	rigid, firm	solid, smooth, powdery and shiny	rigid, smooth
cell membrane	thin, transparent, papery	flimsy, stretchy, clear	thin, clear, shiny	flimsy, stretchy, clear
nucleus	spongy	hard, stone	hard, slight bounce	sponge
chloroplasts	wrapped, layered, soft on hard	flat paper, layered	sponge	sponge
vacuole	flexible water container	flat	hard, slight bounce	powdery, jelly-like

to represent water – the stored water of the vacuole as a lagoon.
Model 1 used the thick rubber as an analogy for being jelly-like. In
each case the students had been involved in the serious work of
thinking about the qualities of sap and how best to represent them
with the resources available to them.

In summary, as Table 7.1 shows, the students' used a range of
textures to represent the different elements of the cell.

Their decisions and selections in relation to texture, shape and
colour expressed meanings which were further shaped by their
incorporation and arrangement of these materials and shapes into
their models. In selecting a material, the students made decisions
which reflected or extended their understanding of a cell. In short,
their selections of texture and shape were motivated, not arbitrary.
The material form and content of their signs wove together to make
meaning.

Imported objects

Some of the students imported a range of ready-formed objects as signifiers with specific histories into their models. In this section we discuss the already-shaped semiotic meanings of imported objects in four models, and the resonant yet transformed meanings of objects through their relocation in the models as a resource for meaning-making and learning.

The vacuole was represented in the textbook linguistically as 'a large space filled with a liquid called cell sap' and represented visually as a large white lagoon shape (see Figure 7.1). The students who made model 2 (Figure 7.3) represented the vacuole by a green water bottle filled with water with green ink in it. They explained their use of the ink as an attempt to thicken and dye the water green. In this way, their representation presents the vacuole as a container and the sap as both more viscuous than water and as a green liquid. We suggest that their choice of a water bottle conveyed meaning by establishing the role of the vacuole in maintaining and storing resources (drinking water). In this context the function of the bottle is as storage and that of the sap is signalled as resource.

The student who made model 3 (Figure 7.4) chose to represent the nucleus with a grey-green stone. Her use of a natural physical object brought with it traces of the context for the existence of the cell. The hard, round stone contrasts with the flatness of the rest of the model. The stone moved as the box was moved, drawing attention to it (and what it represents) through movement and sound. The solid heaviness of the stone produced a slow, controllable movement. The choice of a stone as compared with a marble, assured the stability of the function of control centre as ordered monitoring. The physical nature of the stone, its salience and its potential movement in the box produced its centrality to the model and to what it represented.

Clingfilm was used by several students to represent the cell membrane. It imported meanings of barrier, protection and sterile environments, echoing the students' understandings of the membrane as 'stopping germs and things coming in'. Here, the clingfilm served as a textural analogy (flimsy) and as a functional analogy (barrier).

In another model (not shown here) a student used white sugar cubes and small white buttons to represent the vacuole, and green sweets wrapped in sweet wrappers to represent the chloroplasts. Here we suggest that the imported objects indicated food and stored food.

The representational potentials of culturally shaped semiotic objects are purposefully exploited in the models by the students both in terms of their materiality and the social meanings which they import and express. These objects have the potential to extend the representation of a cell from a material-physical analogy to a social analogy to express and extend students' understanding through material and social analogy, linking them into the wider metaphoric systems of their cultures.

Visibility: Absence and presence

A visual representation is always partial. Here we focus on how 'visibility' can be seen as a meaning-making resource which informed students' learning.

The majority of the students represented all the parts of the cell named in the textbook in their model (cell wall, cell membrane, vacuole, chloroplasts, cytoplasm and nucleus). A few models did not represent all these elements, for example one model represented the nucleus as a hole. The model consisted of a cube made of white paper with a piece of paper inside the cube. Two holes at the centre of the front and back panels of the model revealed the inner section of the model, a sheet of paper with a pencil drawing of a scale pattern. The hole had an essential role in enabling the viewer to see 'inside' the model cell. Through its absence the model emphasized the importance of the nucleus. The student did not represent the chloroplasts, cytoplasm or vacuole as separate elements in her model, rather these elements were represented by the scale pattern. The student transformed each entity into a new sign and in so doing presented the cell as three elements: outside, nucleus as mediator, and inside. We suggest that the absence and presence of parts represented in the students' models is one kind of evidence of what they considered to be significant in their representation of a cell.

The photographic images and the accompanying text in the textbook signalled the microscopic process by which they were made visible. In addition, the arrangement of the diagrams directly below the photographic representations signalled them to be a product deriving from them. Their origin and process of production were made explicit in the arrangement of the page. For some students the shift from image to model signalled a need to carry over the encoded experience of seeing through the use of lids and of windows into the models. As shown in Table 7.2 below, the models varied in the degree to which elements were presented as immediately visible or as to be revealed.

The use of labels in model 2 presented a cell as something which has to be looked into (from above) in order to see its elements. Models 3 and 4 (Figures 7.4 and 7.5) presented a cell as something which is revealed – in the case of model 2 the lid of the box, the outer cell wall, needed to be removed; in model 4 the absence of papier-mâché on the plastic box lid created a window through which to glimpse the inside of the model. By contrast, model 1 (Figure 7.2) represented a three-dimensional cross-section of a cell, presenting it as an immediately visible phenomenon.

The ways in which students constructed visibility in their models served to position the viewer in relation to the model. Model 2 positioned the viewer as an observer outside of the cell looking in. Models 3 and 4 encoded the potential of science to look within, to go deeper. The creation of a window in the lid of model 4 went further as an expression of the experience of looking at a cell through a microscope. Model 1 placed the viewer immediately inside the cell – rather than imbuing the experience of *how to look*, it presented the

Table 7.2 Visibility of elements in the students' models of a cell

	Model 1	Model 2	Model 3	Model 4
Visibility	partial (sill)	lid → revealed	lid with a window → revealed	immediately visible

model-maker and the viewer as *involved in the scientific endeavour of looking*. The different ways in which elements of the cell were made visible encoded the model maker's (and thereby the viewer's) relationship to knowledge and science, as a range of different experiences.

Design

The different ways students chose to frame their cells (e.g. rectangular or circular frames), and their use of texture, shape and colour to realize salience have been discussed in the previous sections of this chapter. Here we focus on how the design of a text and the spatial arrangement of elements produces meaning (Kress, 2000b). The meanings of visual texts can be understood by attending to visual semiotic structures such as composition, the frame of an image and salience (Kress and van Leeuwen, 1996). We discuss two aspects of the students design: centrality and movement *vs.* fixity. Our aim is to be able to discuss the relationships between the elements represented in the students' models of a cell and learning.

Centrality

Centrality is a way of conferring importance on an element. In the textbook (Figure 7.1), the nucleus is represented at the centre of the photograph of the diagram of an animal cell, and at the top right in the representations of a pond weed cell. Some of the students used centrality to confer importance on particular elements (others used colour, size or texture). Model 2 (Figure 7.3) transformed the relationships between elements as shown in the textbook and used centrality to equalize the importance of different elements within the cell: the vacuole was made salient through its size (but it was not foregrounded through the use of colour – it blended in with the other green elements); the nucleus was made prominent through its bouncy texture and use of colour (red); the chloroplasts were made salient through sheer number and the amount of space they occupied. The central space in the model remained empty. This utilization of the central space was also apparent in model 3 (Figure 7.4) where the vacuole occupied the inner, rather than the central, space of the model – the area in which the nucleus could move. In both models centrality was used to create a harmonious symmetry in the relationships between the other parts and within the model as a whole. By contrast, in model 4 (Figure 7.5) the elements were arranged around a central composition to highlight the vacuole and to marginalize the chloroplasts. Centrality was perhaps most significant in the arrangement of the elements within model 1. Here the nucleus was represented as central, both literally and in terms of how the model is held together (through the tension of cotton string between the outer and inner elements of the model). The students drew on centrality as a representational resource for making different kinds of meanings to represent the relationships between elements within the cell as equal or as hierarchical.

Movement vs. fixed

The transformation of the sign 'cell' from the textbook to the students' models enabled the potential for movement. In models 2 (Figure 7.3) and 4 (Figure 7.5) movement was restrained to the movement of the water within the bottle and the bounce of sponge – the elements themselves were fixed within the model. There was more potential for movement in models 1 and 3. The stone in model 3 (Figure 7.4) could move and be removed. The movement of the stone created a strong contrast within the otherwise still model enabling different arrangements of the relationship between the nucleus and the other elements of the model, but fixing the other parts in their spatial positions. Model 1 (Figure 7.2) incorporated the most movement. The whole model rolled and as it did so, the plastic vacuole and white sponge pieces wobbled slightly, changing the shape of the model. That is, the elements of the model stayed in the same relation to one another but they shifted and moved slightly. This movement imbued organic and living qualities on the cell. The fixity of the models carried within it the work of decision about where one element is in relation to another element, and thereby conveyed certainty. In model 3 the movement of the nucleus represented both an interpretation of what it means to be a control centre (i.e. to survey and monitor) and an expression of ambiguity about relations between elements – where is the nucleus in relation to the chloroplasts? Fixity expressed certainty on the part of the model-maker, movement expressed the potential for uncertainty on the part of the viewer. Both can be seen as traces of decision-making and cognitive work on the part of the model-maker.

Materiality and learning

Comparison of the models showed that they can be seen as the product of interested activity, each one a unique transformation of the textbook sign 'cell' drawing on different representational resources and reflecting the cognitive decisions involved in representing a cell as a three-dimensional sign. The models are an expression of *learning as a transformative process* which required the students to engage with thinking and learning in a way that a purely linguistic task would not have required. Linguistically it is enough to say 'the cell has a cell membrane'. To draw a cell membrane involves considerations of thickness of line, depth and medium. To construct a three-dimensional model of a cell membrane involves deciding what it looks like, what material can best represent it, where it is placed in relation to the cell wall, and so on. The construction of the models demanded different work from the students. Our analysis suggests that the decisions required to represent a cell as a visual, three-dimensional entity extended the students' learning well beyond that required by a purely writing-based approach in three key ways.

First, the spatial dimensions of the visual mode demanded consideration of the relationships between the different elements in a more detailed way than the linguistic mode: the visual demands a commitment which the verbal does not. In addition, the shift from two-dimensional to three-dimensional representation opened up different potentials for the representation of relationships between elements through the possibility of layering, representations in depth and texture, and the potential to import pre-existing objects.

Second, the representational potentials of the visual mode (i.e. texture, shape, colour) required the students to think about each of the elements in these terms. In this way, the visual mode demanded that students engage with the functions and qualities of each element in a much more considered way in order to decide how to best represent the entity 'cell'. For example, having to physically represent a part, not just name it, required consideration of issues not present in a linguistically framed task, and issues around representation which would not have been required linguistically.

Third, the visual mode raised a series of questions and decisions regarding how to represent the expression of scientificness, in that the visual resources differed so profoundly from the resources made available linguistically (e.g. the question of what looks 'real', scientific conventions such as simplicity and abstraction, and use of colour).

Our analysis of the models has shown that materiality is a resource available for meaning-making in the science classroom. Materiality can be seen as an expression of students' learning. Focusing on texture, shape and colour enabled us to begin to explore a range of aspects of learning:

(a) The analogies students used to construct the entity 'cell', the features and themes that appeared salient (e.g. containment, and relationships between inner and outer).

(b) How students constructed differences and similarities between elements of the cell and how in doing so the students imbued them with different qualities and functions.

(c) Students' understanding of the function of the elements.

(d) Students' representations of concepts (e.g. control represented as 'brain'), what they considered visually important, and the different ways they expressed this (e.g. through size, colour, shape, centrality).

The shift from text and two-dimensional image to three-dimensional model engaged students in the transformative process of sign-making on the level of mode and on the level of element. We suggest that the selection of communicative mode shapes meaning, that is the 'translation' of meaning between modes has to be seen as simultaneously the transformation of meaning. The application of a social semiotic approach to the students' models of cells demonstrates that the visual and the actional as communication are more than merely illustrative, or a question of fostering student involvement and engagement. Different modes of communication provide different dimensions for meaning-making and this is true for the relations of all modes, action no less than writing. This approach *can* engage students in work, thinking and learning in ways which writing cannot. In short, a social semiotic approach offers a way into understanding the learning potentials of all modes of communication beyond language-as-speech or language-as-writing, and gives access to the range of interests and resources students bring to the learning process.

8

Conclusion

Introduction

We hope that the descriptions of the science classroom which we have provided will have given some insights of a new or different kind and enabled insights which have long existed to be integrated into a coherent framework, so that a new sense of what the *teaching* and the *learning* of science is about may emerge. We think that our approach has something to say about curriculum in demonstrating the integral connection between formal issues of representation (modes and genres for instance) and the *shaping of knowledge* in the terms of our metaphor. We also hope to have pushed at some doors and maybe opened some at least partially. In practical terms, issues that we think are opened for thinking in a new way are questions surrounding pedagogy, curriculum, assessment and teacher education. We also think that we have probed some difficult issues of a theoretical kind in the areas of representation and communication, and perhaps in thinking about the two (hitherto) closely related questions of learning and theories of learning, and language and theories of language quite specifically.

We do not intend to deal with these in any extended sense here at all, but it may be useful to sketch out in the briefest fashion how we see the issues as they are presented by our approach. We have given our descriptions based on what we have seen in classrooms without making any evaluations of what we have seen, since that was not our purpose. Our purpose was to begin to understand the complexity of what goes on. It would also have broken the trust which was the necessary basis on which the teachers so generously permitted us to be observers of what went on and, in truth, we are not now able to make such statements – to do so would require seeing many teachers doing these things. Then a clearer sense of possibilities will emerge of what works under what circumstances and what does not work under any circumstance.

We will deal with these issues under the two headings of *practical issues* and *theoretical issues*. That produces a slight distortion because neither of these is exclusively one or the other.

Practical issues

Pedagogy

The title of the research project on which this book is based is *The Rhetorics of the Science Classroom: A Multimodal Approach*. The term *rhetoric* has become newly fashionable for reasons which may be closely related to the aims of our project. However, our reason for choosing it was not fashionability but rather the sense that a multimodal and social semiotic approach jointly might give us a clearer perspective on what the teacher does, and why s/he does what s/he does at a particular point. The multimodal approach assumes that the different modes have different affordances, and so an entirely new question can be asked: 'What is best communicated using which mode?' If image has affordances which facilitate the communication of spatially organized entities, then it will be no surprise if there has been a move, in textbooks say, to the increased use of images for that purpose. That, of course, is never a full explanation: after all images were available for use before and they were not then used in that way. Nor do we think that technological change alone provides an answer because we know that in certain domains image is not used when it might be.

We also suggest that the materiality of the modes is a crucial matter because it is materiality which determines how we as humans with *bodies* respond to representations in specific modes, and in that lies another aspect of the affordances of modes. Nor can cultural histories be ignored: if in a given culture there is a strongly established relation between mode and content, or mode and genre, for instance, the teacher as rhetor will need to be aware of that. If not, the effectiveness of their teaching is threatened.

The relation of materiality and bodily sensory apperception is an important consideration in teaching in a multimodally aware fashion or, to use our term, in the *design* of the multimodal ensemble. *Design* emphasizes the possibility which exists for the rhetor-communicator of distributing the information and content across different modes: interpersonal aspects may be placed particularly with gesture, intonation, or the use of the body in space. Ideational aspects may be distributed across image, writing or gesture. Textual aspects may be assigned more heavily to syntactic (surface) order, gesture, the body's placement, and so on.

Curriculum

The question of which mode to use for the representation of what content is, of course, closely connected with curriculum. The availability of alternative designs opens the possibilities of choice: through what mode is this part, or this aspect of this part, of the curriculum best represented? Is the structure of an electronic circuit best represented in writing or in image? Is this aspect of the topic of blood circulation best handled using the model of the human body, an abstract image, gesture, or a particular combination of these? As we have shown (in the example of blood circulation) the concept map produces a change in how that curricular content is represented compared to the teacher's request for a 'story' of the journey of a red blood cell around the body. Indeed the genre of concept map using the visual mode is itself open to differing use, one strongly influenced by the underlying metaphor of movement (even if not circular movement), and the other by metaphors of function and hierarchy expressed through spatial proximity and circular arrangements.

There is a large issue here: as the communicational landscape in general is moving more towards the use of image in many domains of communication, especially in popular domains, and as children are more and more habituated to getting information visually, there will be a tendency to follow that trend because not to do so will seem to harbour the danger of not engaging (with) the children's interests.

But changes in mode inevitably bring changes in the representation of knowledge. Whether a change in the representation of knowledge – in our metaphor, in the *shape of knowledge* – amounts to a change in knowledge itself is an issue which our approach raises. The different concept maps produced by the children represent both different arrangements and actual differences in what the content is.

If two of the curricular aims of school science are the transmission of knowledge and the inculcation and habituation of scientific ways of communicating ('talking like a scientist', 'writing like a scientist') then the changes in the communicational landscape will have effects on both of these. That is an issue which will need to be attended to in theory ('Do we wish science content to be changed in this way?') and in practice ('How do scientists now communicate? Which modes and which genres in the various modes do they use as a matter of preference?'). When science content is shifted from representation in writing (and speech) to image (and speech) it may, for instance, change in its representation of cause–effect structures which are more characteristic of (western European) languages and their spoken and written forms than they are of visual representation. The visual may facilitate relations of contiguity rather than relations of cause (the contrast in the children's narratives of blood circulation which make strong use of causal forms – 'the blood got pumped by the heart' – with the concept maps which do not).

Assessment

Much of science teaching now proceeds via the use of image as a full means of communication. Equally, children are expected to represent much of their (learned or discovered) knowledge in visual form. Our admittedly relatively casual observation of assessment and evaluation practices in classrooms shows that teachers tend not to evaluate and assess image in the same way as they do writing. Further, assessment is of course related to learning; it is a metric that relates what has been presented in the classroom/curriculum to that which is observably and demonstrably now part of the student's resources.

Our description of what goes on in classrooms shows that an enormous amount of the curriculum is presented in modes other than speech or writing. If assessment is based on a relation between what has been presented and what is made 'their own' by the children, then at the very least we need to know what it is that is presented. As we have shown, there is a strong 'exchange' or 'trade' between modes, an activity ceaselessly engaged in by the brain. For example, what is presented and taken in via the mode of writing re-emerges represented via the mode of the visual. The materiality of the modes means that children are likely to be differently disposed towards information/ content presented in different modes, that is, they have preferences which are in part cultural and in part physiological. The possibilities for learning are therefore strongly influenced by the modes in which content is presented.

Given that there is trade across modes, and given that the shape of knowledge is transformed in the shift from one mode to another, there is another vast problem here: the teacher or assessment authority may have a specific shape of the knowledge in mind for that particular aspect of the curriculum. In its transduction from one mode into another, say from image to writing, that shape changes. That shift, and the principles of transformation guiding it, may not be overtly recognized by the assessor. Assessment criteria, in other words, may be mode specific, while the common-sense assumption is that they are content specific. Thus assessment needs to be seen and rethought in the context of multimodality.

Teacher education

There is, we assume, little need to say much here. If what we have said so far has any plausibility then it is clear that these are issues which must become part of the curriculum of the education of the science teacher. Science teachers, no less and no more than teachers of other school subjects, see it as their responsibility to cover the science curriculum: their focus is on content. But there are problems with this. Content varies with the variations of form so there is in fact no real possibility of focusing on content alone. From a pedagogic point of view it turns out that teachers of science are engaged in an enormously complex design task: designing (in part on the spot, in part with the aid of long-practised routines) complex rhetorical ensembles composed of different modes. These are constantly redesigned in response to the curricular issue dealt with at that point, but also and perhaps more so, in response to the teacher's perception of how what he or she is doing is getting across to the audience.

The teacher is constantly engaged in the task of assessing students' learning, whether formally or informally. What we have said just above therefore applies with great force to the teacher: how can teachers assess what they are transmitting if they have a notion of communication which fails to focus on much of what is communicated? In particular, teachers must be given the means to become highly reflexive of their practice in this respect, and particularly of the interrelation between modes and shape of knowledge, and between mode and potentials for receptiveness by the students.

Theoretical issues

'Language'

Both in our research project and in this book we have had a dual focus: on the classroom, with a genuine interest in what goes on there communicationally, and on the theory of communication, with a genuine interest in developing a plausible account of human communication anywhere. The science classroom is an exceptionally good place to develop a theory of communication. In part it is simply because the contents of the science curriculum demand a more intense use of a multiplicity of modes of communication to be employed than say the History or the English classroom. Or perhaps it is the conjunction of the discipline of Science, which attempts to reveal that which is not readily perceived by common sense, with the discipline of pedagogy which deals with communication of contents designed by adults for the use of the young. The former lies, semiotically speaking, precisely on the border between culturally unshaped nature and the semiotic resources of the culture. It is no surprise that it should draw on a multiplicity of modes (and their sensory channels) in order to draw nature into the sense of culture and therefore to make the material aspects of communication so much more prominent than they are in many other kinds of communication.

The pedagogic brings the seemingly contradictory problem of making the everyday seem strange so that children will see the need for explanation, and to make the strange accessible to the common-sense dispositions of the young. The first of the two demands estrangement – think of an onion as the site of a scientifically significant phenomenon, think of your heart as a pump, etc. The latter demands the use of metaphors but also of modes which bring the strange back into the realm of the conceivable and connected in the first instance at least to the everyday.

These two aspects bear on the two areas where we think we have opened some paths to further work: theories of language and theories of learning. To take language first. Our approach challenges the deeply entrenched view that language is the central means of communication, that it is a full mode for representation (that everything that needs to be conveyed can be using language), and that everything that can be thought rationally can be expressed in language. In our approach it becomes clear that language, whether as speech or as writing, is only ever a partial means for carrying meaning. But if so, then which aspects of communication and representation does language as speech or writing deal with well (or at all) and which not?

When we are challenged by linguists or applied linguists who say 'This is all very interesting, but I teach language so this doesn't really affect me', our response is that if language does not carry all the meaning in a communicative situation, it becomes crucial to know exactly which meanings it does. This is especially so in contexts where learners learn a second language, since it cannot be taken for granted that the meanings carried by language X in society A will be equivalent to the meanings carried by language Y in society B.

The assumption that communication is always multimodal and that all the modes are fully representational and communicational places a new question against speech and writing as modes and their role in representation and communication. They are partial in both and we need to examine that partiality. The emphasis in multimodality on the materiality of modes also issues a deep challenge to abstract notions of language. Our emphasis throughout on *speech* and *writing* rather than on *language* is one attempt to draw attention to this issue. The materiality of each mode makes it impossible to unify them under one category label.

Learning

A rhetorical approach to communication implicitly but strongly focuses on the effectiveness of the rhetor's actions: has he or she been persuasive? 'Persuasiveness' in teaching equates with the effectiveness of learning. One of our urgent questions therefore was 'What constitutes evidence of learning?' Social semiotics does not ask questions about learning or operate with terms such as 'concept'. These belong to psychology. Semiotics deals with signs, and sign and concept belong to different paradigms of thought and practice. Yet our semiotic approach, which focuses on the transforming activity of the individual sign-maker (transformative in relation to the outwardly visible and available resources of representation as well as in relation to the inwardly invisible mental representations) seems to mirror in some significant ways the notion of concept, conceptual development and so on.

For us the evidence of the transformative action of individuals in their reshaping of resources of representation comes from looking at what happens in the process which starts with the apperception of some aspect of the world, its (hypothesized) transformation in the process of apperception and integration into existing sets of inner representations, the rearrangement of that system or those sets of inner representations in that process, and the transformation that happens in the making of the new sign. Our example of the onion cells is a case in point. In this we take a reasonably strict approach to the concept of transformation, which entails the description of the initial structure(s) and a description of the structures which are the results of the processes of transformation, that is, a description of the structure of the new sign(s). Each aspect of the change in structures is seen as part of the remaking of signs and is therefore significant.

'Learning' for us is then both that process and the reshaping of the internal sets of representations which leave the 'reader' changed in some significant way. Clearly, the focus here is equally on the reshaping of the resources (both external and internal) and on the new arrangement of the inner 'system'. The reshaping of the inner resources leaves the learner as different: he or she can now act differently in representation and in communication.

Throughout the book we have emphasized the effects of the differing affordances of the modes and here we reiterate this in relation to the questions of learning. Four points may be useful to organize this relation of affordances and modes: (i) the physiological aspects; (ii) the cultural and social; (iii) the ontological/epistemological; and (iv) the question of subjectivity in all this. We have already made these points. The physiological aspect focuses on the bodiliness of engagement with the world and its interrelation with the materiality of the modes. There seems to be sufficient evidence to suggest that humans are not all alike in their dispositions towards materiality, sense and engagement with the world. Culture superimposes its own preferences on individual disposition, either furthering and facilitating, or hampering and distorting, as for instance in the question of 'handedness'. Such individual and cultural preferences remain significant: the latter are crucial in multicultural schooling, the former are crucial if the potentials of children are to be fostered. Of course, with considerations of the social come issues of power and its effects on the possibilities of learning.

We have discussed the issues of modes and shapes of knowledge at length and all that is needed here is to draw attention once more to the importance of recognizing this link and to the question of what it is that is learned and in what mode.

Given our brief discussion of learning above, we wish to say here that we see the question of subjectivity in a very similar light, though insisting here that this is always modalized in profound ways by the questions of effect. Of course, some of the things which we wish to bring to the surface of debates around meaning and learning – for instance, materiality and its interaction with sensoriness – begin to touch on this issue. Our notion of 'interest' comes close to, though does not cover except in slight ways, the issue of human desire.

Certainly we wish to challenge and overcome some of the dichotomies which exist still in this area: rationality/emotion and affect, cognition/affect, and the valuations of modes which have supported these. We think that there are significant agendas for work on these issues.

References

Barthes, R. (1968) *Elements of Semiology,* translated by A. Lavers and C. Smith. New York: Hill and Wang.

— (1977) 'The death of the author', in *Image, Music, Text.* London: Fontana, pp. 142–8.

Bateson, G. (1987) 'A theory of play and fantasy', in *Steps to an Ecology of Mind.* Northvale, NJ: Aronson.

Bernstein, B. (1996) *Pedagogy, Symbolic Control and Identity.* London: Taylor and Francis.

Bitti, P. and Poggi, I. (1991) 'Symbolic nonverbal behaviour: talking through gestures', in R. Feldman and B. Rime (eds), *Fundamentals of Nonverbal Behaviour.* New York: Cambridge University Press.

Cope, B. and Kalantzis, M. (eds) (2000) *Multiliteracies.* London: Routledge.

Crook, S. and Taylor, L. (1980) 'Goffman's version of reality', in J. Ditton (ed.), *The View from Goffman.* London: Macmillan.

Crowder, E. M. (1996) 'Gestures at work in sense-making science talk', *Journal of Learning Sciences,* **5**(3): 173–208.

Efron, D. (1972) *Gesture, Race and Culture.* The Hague: Mouton and Co.

Ekman, P. and Friesen, W. (1969) 'The repertoire of non-verbal behaviour: categories, origins, usage and coding', *Semiotica,* **1**(1): 49–98.

Franks, A., and Jewitt, C. (2001) 'The action of learning in the science classroom', *British Journal of Educational Research.*

Freedman, N. (1972) 'The analysis of movement behaviour during the clinical interview', in A. Siefman and B. Pope (eds), *Studies in Dyadic Communication,* New York: Pergamon Press.

Goffman, E. (1974) *Frame Analysis.* Cambridge, MA: Harvard University Press.

Goodwin, C. (1981) *Conversational Organization: Interaction between Speakers and Hearers.* New York: Academic Press.

Greimas A. J. (1987) 'Towards a semiotics of the natural world', in *On Meaning: Selected Writings in Semiotic Theory,* trans. P. J. Perron and F. H. Collins. London: Pinter.

Halliday, M. A. K. (1985) *An Introduction to Functional Grammar.* London: Edward Arnold.

Halliday, M. A. K. and Martin, J. R. (1993) *Writing Science: Literacy and Discursive Power.* London: The Falmer Press.

Hanson, B. (1994) 'The potential of videotape data: emotional correlates of senile dementia in families as a case in point', *Quality and Quantity* **28:** 219–32.

Hodge, R. and Kress, G. (1998) *Social Semiotics.* Cambridge: Polity Press.

Hooke, R. (1667) *Micrographia or some physiological descriptions of minute bodies made by magnifying glasses with observations and inquiries thereupon.* London: James Allestiry, Royal Society.

Kendon, A. (1996) 'Reflections on the study of gesture', *Visual Anthropology* **8**(2–4): 123–31.

Kress, G. (1993) 'Genre as social process', in B. Cope and M. Kalantzis (eds), *The Power of Literacy: A Genre Approach to Writing.* London: Falmer Press.

— (1994) *Learning to Write,* 2nd edition. London: Routledge.

— (1997) *Before Writing: Rethinking the Paths to Literacy.* London: Routledge.

— (2000a) 'Multimodality', in B. Cope and M. Kalantzis (eds), *Multiliteracies.* London: Routledge.

— (2000b) 'Design and transformation', in B. Cope and M. Kalantzis (eds), *Multiliteracies.* London: Routledge.

Kress, G., Ogborn, J. and Martins, I. (1998) 'A satellite view of language', *Language Awareness* 2–3: 69–89.

Kress, G. and van Leeuwen, T. (1996) *Reading Images: The Grammar of Visual Design.* London: Routledge.

— (2001) *Multimodal Discourse.* London: Edward Arnold.

Lemke, J. (1998): 'Multiplying meaning: visual and verbal semiotics in scientific text', in J. Martin and R. Veel (eds), *Reading Science.* London: Routledge.

— (2000) 'Introduction: language and other semiotic systems in education', *Linguistics and Education* **10**(3): 307–34.

Lomax, H. and Casey, N. (1998) 'Recording social life: reflexivity and video methodology', *Sociological Research Online* **3**(2).

Martin, J. (1993) 'A contextual theory of language', in B. Cope and M. Kalantzis (eds), *The Power of Literacy: A Genre Approach to Writing.* London: Falmer Press, pp. 116–36.

Martinec, R. (1997) 'Rhythm in multimodal texts'. Unpublished paper, London Institute of Education.

Mauss, M. (1979) *Sociology and Psychology Essays.* London: Routledge and Kegan Paul.

McNeil, D. (1992) *Hand and Mind: What Gestures Reveal about Thought.* Chicago: University of Chicago Press.

Merleau-Ponty, A. (1969) *The Essential Writings of Merleau-Ponty.* New York: Harcourt, Brace and World.

Myers, G. (1990) *Writing Biology: Texts in the Social Construction of Scientific Knowledge.* Madison: University of Wisconsin Press.

New London Group (1996) 'A pedagogy of multi-literacies: designing social futures', *Harvard Educational Review* **66**(1): 60–92.

Ogborn, J., Kress, G., Martins, I. and McGillicuddy, K. (1996) *Explaining Science in the Classroom.* Buckingham: Open University Press.

Ormerod, F. and Ivanic, R. (1999) 'Texts in practices: interpreting the physical characteristics of texts', in D. Barton, M. Hamilton and R. Ivanic (eds), *Situated Literaces.* London: Routledge.

Scheflen, A. (1974) *How Behavior Means.* New York: Jason Aronson.

Sinclair, J. and Coultard, R. (1975) *Towards an Analysis of Discourse.* London: Oxford University Press.

Sutton, C. (1992) *Words, Science and Learning.* Buckingham: Open University Press.

Vygotsky, L. S. (1986) *Thought and Language,* trans. A. Kozlun. Cambridge, MA: MIT Press.

Wells, G. (2000) 'Modes of meaning in a science activity', *Linguistics and Education* **10**(3): 307–34.

Index